Switched On?
Video Resources in Modern Language Settings

D1630881

MODERN LANGUAGES in PRACTICE

The Modern Languages in Practice Series provides publications on the theory and practice of modern foreign language teaching. The theoretical and practical discussions in the publications arise from, and are related to, research into the subject. *Practical* is defined as having pedagogic value. *Theoretical* is defined as illuminating and/or generating issues pertinent to the practical. Theory and practice are, however, understood as a continuum. The series includes books at three distinct points along this continuum: (1) Limited discussions of language learning issues. These publications provide an outlet for coverage of actual classroom activities and exercises. (2) Aspects of both theory and practice combined in broadly equal amounts. This is the *core of the series*, and books may appear in the form of collections bringing together writers from different fields. (3) More theoretical books examining key research ideas directly relevant to the teaching of modern languages.

Series Editor
Michael Grenfell, *Centre for Language in Education, University of Southampton*

Editorial Board
Do Coyle, *School of Education, University of Nottingham*
Simon Green, *Trinity & All Saints College, Leeds*

Editorial Consultant
Christopher Brumfit, *Centre for Language in Education, University of Southampton*

Other Books in the Series
Cric Crac! Teaching and Learning French through Story-telling
    ROY DUNNING
Effective Language Learning
    SUZANNE GRAHAM
The Elements of Foreign Language Teaching
    WALTER GRAUBERG
The Good Language Learner
    N. NAIMAN, M. FRÖHLICH, H.H. STERN and A. TODESCO
Inspiring Innovations in Language Teaching
    JUDITH HAMILTON
Le ou La? The Gender of French Nouns
    MARIE SURRIDGE
Target Language, Collaborative Learning and Autonomy
    ERNESTO MACARO
Training Teachers in Practice
    MICHAEL GRENFELL
Validation in Language Testing
    A. CUMMING and R. BERWICK (eds)

Please contact us for the latest book information:
Multilingual Matters, Frankfurt Lodge, Clevedon Hall,
Victoria Road, Clevedon, BS21 7HH, England
http://www.multilingual-matters.com

MODERN LANGUAGES IN PRACTICE 10
Series Editor: Michael Grenfell

Switched On?

Video Resources in Modern Language Settings

Steven Fawkes

MULTILINGUAL MATTERS LTD
Clevedon • Philadelphia • Toronto • Sydney • Johannesburg

Library of Congress Cataloging in Publication Data

Fawkes, Steven
Switched On? Video Resources in Modern Language Settings/Steven Fawkes
Modern Languages in Practice: 10
1.Languages, Modern–Study and teaching–Audio-visual aids.
I. Title. II. Series
PB36.F39   1998
418'.0028'4–dec21   98-29753

British Library Cataloguing in Publication Data

A CIP catalogue record for this book is available from the British Library.

ISBN 1-85359-424-5 (hbk)
ISBN 1-85359-423-7 (pbk)

Multilingual Matters Ltd

UK: Frankfurt Lodge, Clevedon Hall, Victoria Road, Clevedon BS21 7HH.
USA: 325 Chestnut Street, Philadelphia, PA 19106, USA.
Canada: OISE, 712 Gordon Baker Road, Toronto, Ontario, Canada M2H 3R7.
Australia: P.O. Box 586, Artamon, NSW, Australia.
South Africa: PO Box 1080, Northcliffe 2115, Johannesburg, South Africa.

Copyright © 1999 Steven Fawkes.

Printed and bound in Great Britain by the Cromwell Press.

Contents

Chapter 1

Opening Titles

BACKGROUND AND RATIONALE

Television and video are a part of everyday life. Programmes are a source of information and of entertainment, and they form a significant part of present day culture, both in the way that they reflect, discuss and illustrate modern life, and in the way that their own content and style shapes what people talk about or the way they behave. Young people in particular look to television and areas of the Press to provide many of the cultural references they need and to keep themselves up to date.

The expansion of access to televisual resources by terrestrial, satellite and cable systems provides a plethora of programming both at home and increasingly in places of learning. For language teachers the improved access to authentic resources from target language speaking countries would seem at first sight to be a life-enhancing development, providing learners with extensive and motivating listening practice in the comfort of their own homes! However, the number of (particularly younger) language learners who will dedicate their own time, of their own free will, to watching television in another language for the good of their souls is not enormous, and the virtue of indiscriminate viewing of programmes has also to be questioned. Our own life experience tells us that a lot of what is broadcast on television is not especially interesting to us personally and does not command the attention of all of our faculties; if we add to this lack of inherent interest the barrier of a different language, then the positive impact of viewing an authentic programme is clearly not guaranteed. Viewers in all sorts of circumstance, then, need to learn, or be taught, to be selective and purposeful about what they watch.

Teachers working with young learners may well be looking into the use of resources on video because of young people's interest in TV itself. The conventions and forms of the medium form part of their culture and so should form an effective addition to the range of resources which a teacher can use. However, there are considerable differences between the sort of viewing carried out by young people in their own time and the sort we may

1

like them to do to support their language-learning at home or in our classrooms. The sporadic and often passive viewing characterised by zapping between channels is probably not most appropriate or constructive, and nor is the use of the television as background noise and movement which only occasionally attracts attention. It is more likely that educational uses of a television resource will involve learners in:

- paying close attention;
- responding to certain cues;
- picking out information or opinions;
- interacting in some other way, either individually or as part of a group activity;
- taking part in some sort of follow-up, which may involve speaking or writing.

The strong message then is that viewing a television resource within a learning context will aim to be active, and is therefore quite different from the sort of passive viewing which may go on in other environments. Learners will need to be encouraged to get the most from the viewing and listening experience and to be trained to use various strategies which will help to this end. These may be strategies for:

- language acquisition
- vocabulary extension
- comprehension
- response
- creativity

and may require careful structuring, consolidation and clarification. This applies especially to young learners, who may need to realise that the bare fact of viewing is not in itself a learning experience.

The implication is that teachers exploiting television resources may well need:

- to educate their learners in how to view;
- to focus their attention;
- to develop strategies which encourage meaningful viewing, with a variety of purposes in mind;
- to encourage interactions between the learners themselves, and between the learners and the resource.

Professor Richard Johnstone gives us a strong message from educational research about the potential for supporting learners' linguistic memory through multisensory routes, of which television can clearly form part:

'There is no doubt that language that is associated with sound, music, movement, colour, drama, and thereby impregnated with meaning, can indeed be assimilated in large chunks.' (Johnstone, 1994)

The purposes of this book are:

- to support teachers in thinking about these principles in terms of classroom practice;
- to suggest some practical strategies for coping with the use of broadcast resources in the classroom from very early stages onwards;
- to investigate a variety of potential learning outcomes;
- to outline suggestions for achieving these outcomes.

Teachers' objectives in investigating the use of broadcast resources either for independent study or in the language classroom may be:

- motivational (trying to interest learners through the resource itself);
- pedagogical (aiming to support learning through a variety of sensory routes);
- cultural (wishing to expose learners to images generated within target language countries);
- linguistic (presenting Native Speaker models of pronunciation, intonation and syntax).

The issues which face teachers wishing to obtain and exploit authentic broadcast resources may include:

- finding out what's on and when;
- finding out what's any use;
- getting hold of it;
- getting time to see it and review it;
- matching it to the language level of the learners;
- finding out how it fits with the scheme of work or teaching programme;
- working out what to do with it;
- recognising when the resource is a primary element of the teaching strategy;
- storing it;
- finding it again when they need it.

These are the sorts of issue which this book will address by considering the rationale and potential value of authentic and purpose-made television in the language classroom within the practical constraints of time, space and energy which attach to all teachers, and by suggesting strategies for the management of such resources and their exploitation with learners in various situations.

THE IDEAL PACKAGE?

What constitutes the ideal teaching resource is of course different for different teachers.

At their best, broadcast resources can provide certain essential elements for the language-learning scenario, with which the teacher and learner can begin to work. The following are desirable ingredients to look out for:

- Stimulus
- Motivation
- Accessible language level
- Quality of language
- Language in context
- Flexibility
- Cultural content
- Ease of use

Stimulus should be available linguistically and intellectually; that is to say that the content or subject matter of the programme (as well as its language) should be of a suitable level of challenge for the audience. The stimulus will provide for receptive understanding of the language contained in the programme in an exposure stage, for replication of that language in a practice stage, and for genuine response to the content matter, which can be exploited at various stages.

Some of this stimulus will ideally take the form of **motivation**, again of different forms. Learners should find the subject matter and style interesting, entertaining or challenging, and should also find the models of language they are exposed to accessible and relevant to their **level** and age. The language content should be largely accessible for language learners, but with an element of unpredictable or extension language to take them forward and to make them feel they are coping with *the real thing*.

The **quality** of a programme resource should be evident in its contribution to the learners' breadth of experience, in its promotion of self-confidence, through presenting language in clear **context**, and in the clarity, wealth and diversity of the linguistic models it presents to its viewers, including excellent models of the target language as used by native speakers. For younger or less confident learners the immediate visual support and illustration offered by a programme resource can be a first step in helping them find their way through a perplexing barrage of extended foreign language input.

To be most useful, programmes need to be **flexible**, including items which are short enough to be dealt with adequately within the strict time-parameters of the classroom or within the attention span of an independent learner working alone. The most useful resources can be used at different levels by learners of different maturity, knowledge or ability.

For some audiences, especially the young, the look of the programme needs to be up-to-date, avoiding the 'cringe factor' of past-it fashions. (For more mature learners, of course, this can sometimes be turned to advantage, as a walk down the sartorial memory lane can provide a good context for practising the past tense, descriptions and the language of opinions.)

Culture is, of course, an essential part of language, and one of the most visible advantages which a television resource naturally has over a printed resource. It can illustrate both explicitly and implicitly how real people behave in real situations and places, offering an experience, sometimes unique in the learners' experience, of 'contact' with native speakers in their own environment (albeit at second hand).

Not all of these ingredients are, of course, always included in the mix of every television resource. Authentic resources in particular will not automatically consider the linguistic level of the foreign language learner, and will consequently need a lot of mediation by a teacher. However, other ingredients may well make up for this with certain learners, who may be very motivated by the idea of coping with totally authentic resources, or who may, indeed, be learning the language for exactly that purpose.

Under the heading of **ease of use** teachers may consider:

- how clearly is the programme titled (or the programme sections labelled)?
- how transparent is what you're supposed to do with it?
- how obvious are the language outcomes?
- how evident are the spots for pausing or interrupting?

A distinctive feature of most language broadcasts specially made for educational purposes is that they have been planned with particular groups of learners (rather than just an indeterminate set of viewers) in mind, and so should be expected to serve their target audience appropriately. They also tend to offer, as well as the programme content itself, supporting resources (often in print) for the teacher to use in planning and to focus the learners' attention on key matters before, during or after the viewing. This may take the form of:

- additional or explanatory information for the teacher;
- key language for the programme;
- a transcription of the programme;
- guidance for the teacher on suggested exploitation strategies for the programme;
- photocopiable or disposable activities for the learners.

Teachers planning to use an educational broadcast may well find it valuable to investigate the existence of such support materials before they start.

While the broadcast resources provided by public television companies are very often free if recorded from air to users in schools and colleges, sometimes a licence is needed. In the UK, for instance, licensing is regulated by a national body called the Educational Recording Agency. Educational institutions often make licensing arrangements for all of their staff which cover recording and use within and sometimes outside the institution, but in any case, teachers are well-advised to check on their rights to use broadcast resources in their own particular circumstances.

As well as transmitting their programmes, some broadcasters publish videotape editions of their resources for sale; regulations for the use of these may very well be different and should be checked. Accompanying printed materials very often have a cost also, and regulations concerning permission to make photocopies of these must also be checked individually.

The first steps in identifying useful, if not ideal, packages are in:

- considering what ingredients we are looking for to supplement or replace resources we already have;
- locating what resources exist;
- evaluating their contents;
- identifying what and how they can contribute to the language-learning experience we aim to provide.

Chapter 2
The Big Picture

USING VIDEO RESOURCES

In 1997, the Schools Curriculum and Assessment Authority (SCAA), the UK body charged with overseeing implementation and practice of the National Curriculum, published guidance for teachers on managing the National Curriculum Programmes of Study. It made specific references to the contributions to be made to the teaching and learning of a foreign language by educational broadcast resources, particularly in the areas of:

- communicating in the target language;
- developing language skills;
- developing learning skills and knowledge of language;
- developing cultural awareness.

Research from the National Foundation for Educational Research suggests that broadcasts can support not only specific language skills, but broader cognitive developments as well (Sharp, 1995):

> 'Through their stimulating content and presentation, broadcasts were felt to contribute to learning by enhancing attention, motivation and recall of factual information. As well as conveying information, broadcasts were found to be helpful in teaching pupils skills and developing their conceptual understanding.'

and that less academically successful learners may find particular advantages:

> 'As head of the audio-visual research group at the Open University (OU), Bates points out that a TV representation can provide a bridge between the abstract and the concrete, or between personal experience and abstraction. In his opinion, TV examples of this kind are most helpful for borderline candidates.

> The suggestion made by previous researchers (Bates, 1981; Kozma, 1991) that the ability to make connections between real phenomena and

theoretical concepts is a particular strength of television as a learning medium.'

while, in relation to language learning specifically the provision of images alongside words again offers great support for the less-experienced or less able learner. Guenther Mueller and Rick Altman find that while better learners get sufficient clues from the language, beginners benefit greatly from visual support:

'In the case of those students for whom a contextual visual appears to enhance listening comprehension, seeing the visual before hearing the passage seems to result in the greatest amount of listening comprehension recall. This "visual before" treatment was most effective for one or more of the following reasons:
(1) the visual serves as an advance organiser;
(2) in seeing the overall context first students were less likely to formulate wrong hypotheses and consequently better able to guess the meaning of unfamiliar words and phrases;
(3) seeing the visual before hearing the passage heightened the students' interest and caused them to pay close attention to the passage.' (Mueller, 1980)

'It has been repeatedly demonstrated that even a single line drawing that provides only a very general indication of the contents of a passage can have a marked effect on comprehension, if it is shown to subjects before they read or listen to the passage. Surprisingly even pictures only vaguely related to a passage aid comprehension more than prior access to a list of the actual vocabulary words employed in the passage.' (Altman, 1989)

The NFER research found that UK language teachers recognised the following specific gains among their learners of modern languages (Sharp, 1995):

Listening skills   61%
Understanding life in other countries 42%
Oral skills   33%

Yet these desirable outcomes are not automatic; such gains require consolidation and planned development. Some of the teacher's purposes for using programme resources can be tabulated as shown on the following page (with some questions in parentheses):

Listening training	Familiar language in different contexts.
Language development	Gradual inclusion of some new language in a clear context for interpretation.
	(How formal/informal should this interpreting be?)
Extending listening	Closer to a real life experience, developing confidence about coping with the unexpected.
Speaking training	Excellent/varied models of native speakers.
	Illustrations of natural variations in formulating phrases.
	Natural inclusion of dynamic bits of language.
Cultural background	Authentic behaviours, body language and facial expressions, scenes of real life, contrasts in habits.
	(How explicitly should this be explored?)
Extending range of material and of input	Different angles on core language/topics.
Basis for creative work	Writing and speaking.
Motivation	

FIRST STEPS

Effective language learning often relies upon interaction. At different stages learners may have different imperatives, from striving to accumulate vocabulary, to understanding and applying structure, to reproducing accurate pronunciation, to developing their control of idiom, but one of the core strategies they may employ for all of these will reside in types of interaction which present new language and encourage comprehension, which give scope for language practice and response, and which create an audience for genuine language performance. This interaction may be:

- between the learner and other people (the teacher and the rest of the class);
- between the learner and the learning resources (books, tapes, broadcast resources);
- between the learner, the resources and learning strategies;
- or between other combinations of these.

It follows that there are key roles for the teacher introducing a new resource. These lie in:

- the initial evaluation of that resource;
- the subsequent planning of activities relevant to particular learners, to established methodology and to the syllabus;
- experimentation with using the resource; and
- subsequent analysis of what was or was not effective.

Investigation of new teaching resources and different methodologies can arise from various imperatives: the need to fill a curriculum gap, the urgency of catering for a particular teaching group or individual or ongoing curriculum or methodological development.

Initial selection of interesting resources often arises from professional conversations with colleagues, and can usefully focus on particular issues of general concern:

'What do you use with your top/lower ability group?'
'Have you found anything really useful for conveying cultural information?'
'I'm looking for something really motivational ...'.

Having said that, nothing is more valuable than personal experience. Experimenting with any new resource, including television, in order to 'cope with' a particular class or requirement of the timetable is a high risk activity, as the teacher may be working from a situation of inexperience with the hardware and unfamiliarity with the resource, and may be impelled by an external directive. All of this can lead to a lack of confidence or conviction for the teacher and present certain types of class with an irresistible temptation to react badly. The sight of the TV and video in the classroom is not an automatic way to reach the class's heart, or to produce attentiveness or tolerance towards technological problems!

Screen tips
Don't expect the sight of a TV in class to produce automatic reactions of sunshine and light!
Avoid saying 'Today we're going to do something nice.' It undermines your position from the start.

Picture the scene
Class Z, unprepared, waiting at their desks at the end of the afternoon, casually chewing on the corners of their textbooks. In walks the teacher, wheeling the video trolley ... 'Today we're going to ...' It could be the equivalent of 'Light the blue touchpaper!'

It is more comfortable, then, to try out a new resource or approach from a base of being well-prepared and with a receptive class. In this situation the teacher starts from a position of confidence, and the focus can be on the methodology of exploiting the resource, rather than classroom management issues.

It is often helpful also to prepare the class in advance, in order to contain their excitement, and to choose a time of day and a time in the week when they are likely to be most receptive.

As with all things it is advisable for a teacher using a new resource for the first time to start with a small-scale project, working with a class where there is at least the likelihood of a positive response, and identifying areas of success and problematic issues for subsequent investigation.

> - Choose your group.
> - Prepare them in advance.
> - Choose your time.

PREPARATION

At the outset it is important to remember that different groups of learners respond in very different ways to similar approaches (and similar resources). An activity which works brilliantly well with one class on one day can fall completely flat on the next day with a parallel class, and indeed a similar activity can fail to grab the attention of the same class in different circumstances. We, as teachers, should therefore think about evaluating a particular teaching resource with reference to our knowledge of a specific audience and to our relationship with that audience. This applies as much to using television or video programmes as it does to any other resources or approaches.

Choosing a teaching resource can be a very personal thing and in the area of television resources in particular the personal taste of the teacher can be critical in the selection, presentation and effective use of the programme. Clearly, as the mediator of the programme, it is important for the teacher to present it in a positive light to the class, but this does not mean that the teacher can only use programmes that she/he personally admires.

On the one hand it is essential that the teacher is confident with the programme content as well as the hardware and classroom management issues involved in using a programme; on the other, individual taste should be balanced carefully with the likely response of the class or teaching group to the programme, as this is the primary issue under consideration.

In other words, the questions to ask are:

'*How will* **they** *(the learners) respond to this?*' *or*
'*How can I get them to respond to this?*'

A great issue to bear in mind is that of **time**, both time in the classroom and time in the preparation phase. For the purposes of a curriculum development project it is usually safer to keep the time constraints very much under control. Rather than committing several weeks of classroom time to using the whole of a particular series, with no guarantee of successful response or outcomes, it is often more effective to try out a much smaller scale project, maybe even within one lesson. This clearly requires much less teacher time for evaluation, preparation of ancillary resources, thinking about inter-actions and subsequent review. It also serves to focus the attention more sharply on the particular responses of the learners and issues that need to be reconsidered.

- Choose your time.
- Choose your resource.
- Plan.

Even within the single lesson project it is helpful to have a back-up plan just in case something does not work out as envisaged: if the video player has been 'borrowed' by a colleague or is out of order, or if the class is in upheaval because of the imminence of an inoculation, or if they say 'We saw this last year'.

In summary:

Screen tips
Start small-scale
Ask what other people have used
Select a teaching group who you think will respond
Get them ready
Work within a time limit
Get yourself ready
Have a back-up plan
Stay confident

EVALUATION

Getting hold of programmes, setting up the systems that accompany their use, managing equipment and planning specific lessons all require energy and time; so the teacher will wish to be convinced of what a particular programme (or indeed any other teaching resource) can offer in the classroom. This contribution may be in terms of the headings given above or may be additional or unique criteria relevant to the individual school, class or teacher.

In selecting a resource the teacher may be influenced by:

- promotional literature about a new resource;
- personal recommendation from a colleague;
- professional advice.

As is often the case, word-of-mouth recommendation can be a very positive indicator, as colleagues who recommend a resource will often have used it effectively themselves and will be able to describe how to use it very practically. The more professional recommendations, though, may pick out interesting and relevant features of resources in a broader context which a colleague in the fray of day-to-day teaching may have overlooked.

Ultimately, there is nothing to beat personal evaluation, and actually working with a resource yourself. This sort of evaluation can be problematic as an individual's own aesthetic judgments may become entangled with professional ones. So, the following questions can be of help during a first viewing of a programme in focusing attention on the target group(s) with whom it might be useful. Not all of the headings will be relevant to particular situations or resources, and, for this reason a condensed photocopiable version of this Evaluation Schedule is included in Chapter 8 on page 76, along with a worked example of how it might be completed on page 77.

If a whole teaching department is involved in a project, it is suggested that a copy of this sheet can be filed in the departmental resource bank for other colleagues' use. This can contribute to subsequent discussion if the resource is considered to have earned a place in the agreed scheme of work.

Detailed Evaluation Schedule (*with commentary*)

General

Title of the programme/series:

Target age (if stated):

If a target age is not stated, what seems likely?

The information above is critical and the identified target group should be borne in mind when the relevance of the items below is checked.

Stimulus

One of the key questions in working with any sort of authentic or semi-authentic material is what sort of stimulus it provides the viewer with.

Does it provide good and clear models for replication?

Does it allow for easy interruption for explanation, repetition or questioning?

Does it provoke learners to wish to interrupt themselves to ask questions or add comments?

Motivation　.

A programme can present different sorts of motivational features (music, drama, animation, content, humour).

Will the overall design of this programme appeal to the target group of learners?

Is it an appropriate style or genre?

Does it provide a range of different speakers?

Are the people in the programme interesting?

Does it provide core language in formats other than plain speech?

i.e. drama, song, verse, narrative.

Level

Does it fit with the maturity level of the teaching group?

Is the language level largely appropriate to the target group?

Does it include any in-built repetition?

This may be important for some teaching groups, and will have implications for how the programme is used with them.

Quality

Are the examples of the target language relevant and clear?

Does the programme present good models of pronunciation and intonation?

Does it feel like a 'real' programme?

Context

Do the visual elements help clarify the language appropriately through context clues?

Does the programme offer any support for comprehension in the form of writing?

(e.g. subtitles or captions)

Flexibility

Is the content of the programme relevant to the scheme of work and/or the learners' needs and interests?

Are the segments of the programme of the right length for this group?

Would sections of the programme interest other teaching groups?

Culture

Is the programme clearly sited in the target language culture?

Are the images supportive of developing cultural awareness?

Are the cultural images in line with what the teacher/ the department aims to present?

Ease of use

Are the programme segments clearly labelled?

Other criteria

These may relate to general issues such as gender balance or the multicultural mix, or to particular issues such as the use of 'pieces to camera' which allow for close viewing of lip movements.

Clearly such evaluation will need to take into account **planning issues** at several levels. At the macro level the resources will need to show how they fit with, and what contribution they will make to the long-term scheme of work:

- What skills will they contribute to?
- What attitudes will they contribute to?
- What experiences will they offer?
- What insights will they offer?
- How will they enhance the learner's achievement or performance?

This analysis of the place of the resource in a long-term process enables the teacher to identify at what points in the learners' progress they will have access to certain experiences. It may, for instance, be the policy of a teaching department that language learners should have access to a certain amount of authentic speech from native speakers in each year of their study, and that exposure to video resources can contribute to this.

For instance:

End of First Year:	Viewing five educational magazine TV programmes. First whole class session(s) with Foreign Language Assistant.
Second Year:	Viewing five educational magazine TV programmes. Whole class and smaller group sessions with Foreign Language Assistant. Optional Study Visit abroad.
Third Year:	Viewing five educational drama TV programmes (for motivation). Whole class and smaller group sessions with Foreign Language Assistant, preparing tests. Hosting visitors in school on Study Visit.
Fourth Year:	Viewing five drama TV programmes; five culturally-based programmes. Independent listening to audiotapes. Optional exchange abroad.
Fifth Year:	Viewing ten syllabus-related video resources for revision, vocabulary-enhancement. Viewing short authentic resources from satellite channels related to syllabus. Intensive speaking practice with Foreign Language Assistant.

At the other end of the planning scale the running of individual lessons will also need to be considered in the evaluation phase, as the teacher's involvement in producing interactive learning activities based on the resources will be instrumental in actually making the most of the experience. These activities can be many and varied; some potential outcomes are explored in the next chapter.

WHY KEEP RESOURCES ON TAPE?

Once the potential of a particular broadcast resources has been identified, practical issues come into play.

Most television resources are used in classrooms from videotape, for a variety of reasons. Firstly, it is very unlikely that a programme which fits with a particular timetabled lesson will be broadcast at exactly the time of that lesson, and secondly, live use of a programme severely limits the type and amount of interaction which learners can have with and around the resource.

Picture the scene

The class is viewing a sequence of advertisements live on the Satellite channel, when there is a particularly useful linguistic construction which the teacher wishes to draw attention to.

Teacher's options	**Class response**
Talk to the class over the ongoing broadcast.	Ignore the teacher!
Switch off the broadcast.	Frustration.
Switch off the sound.	Continue to watch the silent pictures, still ignoring the teacher.

However, if the adverts were on videotape, the teacher could return to the selected item later in the lesson, or indeed play the item at the start of the viewing in order to raise awareness. Furthermore, the item is still available on tape subsequently if more detailed analysis or drilling is required, whereas the broadcast version of the advert may not come back into the live schedule again for several hours, if at all.

Secondly, in order to use the resource most effectively the teacher will wish to view it personally, consider which points will be most interesting for the class to observe and respond to, and what the teaching sequence will be. It is advisable for the teacher to watch the whole of the programme at least once, in order to be fully aware of what the learners will see and hear, to spot opportunities and to predict what problems may arise, either linguistically or otherwise, for the viewers.

Such detailed pre-viewing may be speeded up by prior reference to the transcript of the programme, where this is available.

Some broadcast resources have only an evanescent life; they are relevant and useful for a very short period of time. A news programme for instance will lose its impact after the first day of transmission, and watching great weather reports of the past does not sound like a very stimulating activity!

Programmes with such necessary immediacy will have appeal and relevance to certain groups of learners, so it may be most appropriate for the teacher to designate a particular 'topical' videotape for the temporary storage of such resources. This tape can then be used very soon after recording with relevant classes or sent home for independent viewing and then re-recorded.

Other sorts of programme however have a much longer life-expectancy, and many are purposely designed not to lose their topicality too soon. Educational resources, for instance, are often planned to have a repeat life of several years, and try therefore not to be linked to specific events or style issues which will soon expire. These resources are designed, for the most part, to be used from tape, giving the teacher and learner the greatest flexibility in viewing, replaying and reviewing the programme over a period of time.

Practical questions connected with using, storing and maintaining tapes are discussed in Chapter 6: 'Changing Channels'.

The question of **when** to incorporate a video resource into the teaching plan has several levels. If the viewing is being used only as a reward or a temporary release from 'real work' the time implications will be quite different from the situation where specific motivation or stimulus is being exploited. In this latter case 'when' may involve the following:

- in terms of an individual learner or a specific class it will be important to think of the time of day and their consequent state of mind;
- in terms of the linguistic content we will need to consider the stage learners have reached in the learning process;
- and in terms of the outcomes we are looking for we will need to situate the use of the programme within the precise teaching sequence.

The range of such outcomes is considered in the next chapter.

Chapter 3
Finding the Wavelength

'Research into the effectiveness of broadcasts supports the importance of the adult's role in helping children learn from TV. ... In a small-scale study, Choat and Griffin (1986b) evaluated the effects of teacher intervention before and after viewing programmes in a schools TV series. The group whose teacher had provided preparation and follow-up of the programmes made the greatest gains in tests of comprehension and inference.' (Choat & Griffin, 1986, quoted in Sharp, 1995)

Television is looked at by some teachers as a great motivator, because of its association with relaxation and the atmosphere of home. In the domestic context television viewing may be rather passive, providing background noise and images and frequently requiring only low-level response. The learning situation is different, and there is considerable potential for the teacher to explore a wide range of outcomes from a programme, by tuning in to the responses of the class.

It may be that, for students in the early stages of learning a language, the pleasant ambience of TV viewing *will* be used largely to motivate and support. After all, inexperienced language learners are coming to terms with the sounds, structures meanings and feel of a foreign language, all at the same time, and for many, as Eric Hawkins says:

'Linguistic tolerance does not come naturally ... The first reaction to language that cannot be understood is suspicion, frustration, even anger.' (Hawkins, 1984)

This obstacle is one that some learners find very difficult to get over, but for which the reassurance of a familiar television experience may provide the necessary impetus.

Television viewing is associated with entertainment and relaxation, which are no bad things in themselves, but which, for teaching purposes, need to be built on by the mediating teacher in order to produce a useful interaction for a class of learners.

On the one hand it is valuable for learners to be in a relaxed frame of mind for the acquisition of certain sorts of information and experience; on the other it is important that some stimuli are highlighted for immediate response and reaction, in order to develop, for example, critical or observational faculties.

Maintaining initial enthusiasm is critical. If the propensity of a learner is to link the viewing of a programme with enjoyment, this propensity still needs to be consistently reinforced by the teacher's follow-up.

Picture the scene
The class is interested to see the video equipment in the classroom, and enjoys watching the introduction of a gameshow in the target language. The teacher then stops the tape and writes up comprehension questions based wholly on the linguistic content of the programme:

What was the first competitor's name?
Where did she come from?
What was funny about the joke she told?

The impact on the class's enjoyment might be considerable!

Some issues may be:

- The class may not have considered that they needed to be memorising details from the show. (This is not what they would do in their 'real life' viewing after all.) Consequently they are now stressed.
- The style of the follow-up activity turns the programme format into a text to be interpreted like any other piece of text, without building on its uniqueness.
- In particular, the whole of the visual stimulus is ignored.
- The emphasis on comprehension turns the viewing into a test.

In order to retain learners' initial interest in using a TV resource, the follow-up activity which they are asked to undertake must be appropriate to the style of the programme, and must have some related element of enjoyability; after all, if the *task* we present is tedious or difficult the nature of the original *text* is immaterial.

So it is important to consider the particular strengths and qualities of televisual resources in order to be able to develop strategies for their exploitation which are both appropriate and effective. Such strategic development *may* begin from considering the programmes purely as visually supported listening resources, but should also recognise that they have the potential to offer more than simply audio with pictures, and that interaction with them can produce unique situations where language need, language manipulation and consequent language learning can take place.

Students may be stimulated, for instance:

- to check their understanding of what has been viewed;
- to imitate or replicate;
- to ask for clarification or repetition;
- to personalise, by borrowing language from the programme;
- to try to offer an opinion or reaction;
- to relate what they have seen to their own experience through an anecdote;
- to view and listen solely for pleasure;

and any of these real responses can create a need to produce meaningful language through manipulating what has been presented and what has been learnt previously or through seeking new means of expression.

USING TELEVISION WITH PUPILS OF A WIDE ABILITY RANGE

As with all sorts of teaching resources, television programmes are there to be used as and when the teacher thinks appropriate. One of their particular qualities is that they can be used to meet a number of objectives, depending on the age and character of a particular teaching group.

Another is that they can draw and focus the attention, as found in the NFER research quoted above. Features associated with higher levels of attention (Sharp, 1995) include:

- changes in scene
- movement/action
- dramatic content
- film of animals
- partially clad people
- cartoons and animation
- visual effects
- visual detail/close up
- lively/dramatic music
- sound effects
- female voices

Not all of these features (e.g. partially clad people) will be present in many language resources, of course!

When working with young learners of low ability a television resource may be particularly appropriate as it does not have the inherent barrier of text which printed resources often confront learners with very early on. An objective with such a teaching group could be wholly *experiential* if the act of viewing a short clip is as much as the group could cope with, or if the group is developing skills of concentration.

At a different level a television programme may be used in order to provide *real, multisensory experiences* through the combination of visual background (e.g. a real place elsewhere in the world), visual foreground (the body language, facial expression, conventions and appearance of real people on film), sound (in the form of voices, music, background noise) and sometimes graphics to support understanding. This is particularly the case with some *cultural* details. A programme filmed on location in a target language country can provide a rich combination of sight and sound, which can be complemented by classroom activities involving physical move-ment, manipulation, touch and, where appropriate for the learners, smell and taste.

Alternatively or additionally, the programme might be used to *encourage contributions* from the class, reactions to the places or people seen, recognition of particular visual or, of course, spoken language items.

This could well lead to *participative use*, in which the group imitates or replicates some of the items featured in the programme, joining in with a song, for example or making their own version of a short conversation or presentation.

Features associated with pupil involvement (Sharp, 1995) include:

* songs
* modelling of actions pupils can emulate
* humour
* questions/predictions
* controversial statements
* surprising events and information

Linguistic objectives are available at a variety of levels which can be adjusted to the level of the learners and range from the recognition of which person is speaking, through discernment of individual lexical items to their replication and adaptation to personal needs, and beyond that.

Reinforcement for language previously acquired can be achieved by spotting familiar words or phrases in new or different contexts, and this in turn can be the basis for practice activities in which pupils manipulate structures and vocabulary they already know.

Similar issues and objectives are, of course, relevant to learners of all ages and abilities. To get the most from a resource with a class of any age or ability level, it is important for the teacher to consider particular planning issues:

- Why am I using it?
- What do I want out of it?
- Which bit do I use for this purpose?
- What preparation will the class need?
- What interaction will there be?
- What follow-up will there be?

This planning schedule is also in the photocopiable Chapter 8 on page 78 for use in detailed lesson planning.

Of these the question of teacher and learner interaction with the programmes is particularly important, as this is what can create a significant impact and generate much communication and language use. This interaction may involve:

- direct physical response to what is seen or heard;
- manipulation (e.g. of flashcards or other visuals);
- completing a worksheet;
- pausing the tape for explanation or elaboration;
- repeating a section;
- predicting before viewing;
- commenting or recapitulating;
- asking or answering questions;
- extending;
- comparing what happens in the programme with the first-hand experience of pupils.

Why am I using it? What do I want out of it?

These questions will determine how the programme is used and which strategies for follow-up are most relevant.

Programmes can be useful in supplying an initial context for the lesson, setting the scene and conveying an atmosphere of the target language environment, or alternatively can be used to revisit or consolidate a topic by illustrating it in a new context.

A television series uses the combination of colour, sound and often music in order to provide a rich experience, which can be linked with active participation in the classroom (movement, display, cross-curricular work).

Additional visual resources for use on flashcards, pairwork cards, computer overlays or overhead transparencies can be used for pupils to handle and manipulate, put in sequence, match to the screen or use as mnemonics and prompts for subsequent speaking work.

Much cultural information is included in visual montages, and in the background of scenes. In order to explore them the teacher may well wish to show a clip several times, maybe using the pause button to pick out a particular detail for discussion.

Which bit do I use for this purpose?

It is not always essential, or indeed desirable or helpful, to use the whole of a programme uninterrupted from start to finish. It may be that only one short section deals with exactly the topic in hand and provides the core of a substantial piece of work for the class.

It may be that the programme revisits the core topic or language at more than one point, in which case it may be appropriate to view the whole thing; alternatively it may be more efficient in terms of available time to edit the programme tape in order to have the two relevant sequences close together. (In this latter case it is important to check that your establishment's recording arrangements allow you to do this before you start.)

What preparation will the class need?

When pre-viewing a programme with a particular class in mind, the teacher will be aware of certain language items or structures with which the learners will be unfamiliar, and will need to make judgments about whether these will be:

- comprehensible from the context;
- not especially significant or likely to worry the class;
- in need of presentation in order to maintain the viewers' confidence.

Presentation may then take a form with which the class is familiar: flashcards, wordlists, transparencies, illustrations, etc., which can, of course, be recycled in the follow-up phase.

What interaction will there be? What follow-up will there be?

Some features of programmes invite direct interaction, such as questions, songs, games and competitions. Even where the structure of a programme does not invite such direct reaction, teachers can devise very active experiences by exploiting the technology of the video player: pausing the tape, rewinding, replaying more slowly or with the sound off, or hiding the picture in order to focus on sounds.

Active responses may range from sequencing of picture cards or manipulating wordcards, through choral chanting to running dictation, dramatic reconstruction or competitive memory games, using visual montages or paused scenes for the stimulus.

The power and range of the visual images themselves can help in getting a group to respond through their direct appeal, and can lead naturally into extension work. The initial response can be at a variety of levels including:

- simple observation;
- comparison with the pupil's own experience;
- comparison with other images on screen or with real objects and visuals in class;
- description of a scene or a process;
- offering of comments;
- sequencing;
- making notes (by a range of means, not necessarily writing);
- further reference or reading.

The visual nature of TV programmes also provides many opportunities for follow-up work involving display or modelling. For example, interviews and spoken presentations on screen adapt well to similar activities which make natural links between the language skills. Within groups or as individuals learners can:

- produce a short or detailed version of the monologue/dialogue *in writing*;
- *read* a related text;
- create linked prompts or visual aids (for subsequent display);
- enact their new presentation *in speech*.

Similarly on-screen demonstrations of methods provide stimulus for direct physical response (in the form of following the instructions) and also potentially for response in the form of sequencing or of giving instructions, by creating a similar demonstration on a different topic.

Television materials can then be used at different stages in the language learning sequence, for:

- introducing a new topic or language;
- consolidating a known topic or language;
- presenting known language in a different context;
- illustrating a cultural point or extracting cultural information;
- supplementing other material in a direct and engaging way;
- stimulating a variety of responses;

and our objectives for using television programmes in language teaching may include:

- developing (or testing) listening skills;
- speaking skills;
- language development;
- cultural awareness;
- creative work in speech or writing.

Whatever aims apply to using a particular item with a particular class, the learning objectives and appropriate classroom activities will be accordingly different, in order to focus on particular language skills.

LISTENING SKILLS

One of the unique qualities of a television resource is its combination of aural and visual inputs, allowing unconfident learners to develop strategies for coping very straightforwardly through their use of context clues.

A programme about shopping, for instance, may very well illustrate the shop that is being discussed, along with close-ups of items for sale, and relevant signs and notices which support comprehension while the dialogue is proceeding. At an initial level this allows the learner to identify the topic in hand very readily and then to begin to focus on the core spoken language itself by identifying the key words, isolating them, repeating them, and beginning to use them. The implication is clearly that viewers may need several exposures to such examples in order to extract the maximum.

At the same time as they focus on the language viewers will be noticing cultural details, possibly in the background of the camera shot. Whether these are made explicit or not is in the control of the teacher, and this matter is discussed below.

What are the listening skills we wish to develop with the wide range of learners in our classes? And what sort of strategies could we apply to broadcast resources in order to develop them?

In the following chart the context of *listening* is enhanced by the presence of visual input.

Listening skills to be developed	Strategy for learners to try
Paying attention to the person speaking	Listening and viewing
Interest in other people	Listening and commenting, asking questions
Responding to what is heard	Listening and doing something
Enjoying listening	Listening for pleasure with no task
Identifying pronunciation and intonation	Listening and rehearsing
Judging mood, feelings and relationships	Listening and reacting Listening and describing
Guessing and predicting	Listening after a brainstorm Using the visual cues and context
Coping with distractors and fillers	Extended listening to authentic conversation with visual support
Gist comprehension	Listening and selecting keywords from a multichoice list
Picking out detail	Listening and checking or completing a transcript
Perseverance	Listening to a longer text, in order to review (and not interpret) it.
Linking the spoken and the written word	Listening and following a transcript
Remembering	Listening and rebuilding a text Listening and performing
Explaining, making a résumé or digest	Listening and note-taking Transposing from spoken to written language

These strategies are developed in example activities in Chapter 7.

LANGUAGE DEVELOPMENT

Although the most immediate relevance of using programme resources may be in motivation or authenticity or in the provision of supported and comprehensible input, other aims and objectives may be relevant also.

Issues of **progression** and self-confidence are supported, starting from the learners' recognition that the flood of foreign language makes sense and moving through some of the following, sometimes with the teacher's intervention:

- learners picking up the sense of the language from the pictures;
- identifying that a lump of language stands for a particular meaning;
- replication of that lump of language;
- identification of particular sounds within the lump of language;
- picking out key words or phrases:
- linking to written form of the word;
- practice in recombining of phrases and words.

SPEAKING SKILLS

The core language presented by the programme provides models for imitation and adaptation, but the content of any programme is more than the sum of the words used within it, and it may well be that it is this combined content which will be the stimulus for productive speaking work in the target language.

Programme stimulus =	Spoken language +
	Issues explored +
	People seen +
	Graphics +
	Images +
	Viewers' responses

At a first level, there are opportunities for the viewer simply to repeat a significant section of the language they have heard. This may be for purposes of pronunciation or intonation practice (i.e. getting a feel for the sounds of the language) or in order to allow the viewers to get a sense of what the speaker is saying by saying it for themselves (i.e. the meaning of the language).

At another level the producers of the programme have selected issues or themes liable to interest their audience; these issues may in themselves provide the substance for classroom responses or discussions. At the same time, the visual element of the programme must not be ignored, as it is very often this, in 'real life', that stimulates genuine gossip or conversation after the viewing of a television programme. Speaking work could therefore usefully focus on the '*Did you see ...?'* sort of conversation we often overhear or participate in.

Linguistically this opens up areas to do with description, opinion-giving, question-asking, exclamations and narrative which can be pitched at an appropriate level for the language learners involved.

Often teachers wish to develop their students' ability to answer (and also to ask) questions, and they therefore frequently base activities on the **comprehension** of a 'text', by putting the focus either on detail or on gist. With a television resource the potential for questioning is expanded as the type of questions used by the teacher can be broader than those simply related to the *language* of the text; they can embrace the *situation* surrounding the speakers, their *appearance, lifestyle* issues and many less visible aspects also, such as *mood, personality* and *relationships*. These may not be explicitly discussed in the programme, as even in the most two-dimensional soap operas characters are not often reduced to saying '*I am angry*'! However, if they fit with a topic in the current teaching scheme, such language themes can be easily accessed from a genuine context.

Speaking work can be linked to what people do in real life after viewing a programme. In other words the learners can be asked not only to locate answers within the spoken text, but also to use their more general skills and knowledge about life, people and situations to speculate on a wider range of issues. Clearly, in order to do this, they will need to have some preliminary language to use, but this language may well appear somewhere in the syllabus anyway, and can be built into a scheme of work alongside relevant topic language at suitable points. (The appropriateness of particular functions will, of course, depend on the nature of the particular programme being exploited.)

Sample progressive language functions for discussing a TV programme			
	Beginners	**Intermediate**	**Advanced**
Opinions	Like/dislike	Adjectives Comparisons	Justifying opinions
Describing places	Using nouns	Adding adjectives	Making contrasts
Describing people	Size Clothes	Personality Physical appearance	Anecdote Hypothesis
Questions asked by learners	*Based on observation*	*Based on interpretation*	
	What colour ...? Where ...? Who ...?	What did ... say? What is ... like?	What do you think? Why ...?

READING

Although reading would seem to be a minor element of the broadcast resource. authentic television programmes often contain a surprising amount of on-screen text:

- titles and credits;
- headlines in news and current affairs programmes;
- maps;
- pack shots in advertisements;
- questions in quiz or game shows;
- authentic signs and notices in streets.

Because all of these are placed in context, their recognition and decipherment can have more meaning for the viewer who discovers them. Additionally, purpose-made educational programmes will make selective use of written captions to highlight or explain particular things; these may well involve core linguistic items such as questions, and should be drawn to the attention of learners who may well wish to use them themselves.

Some programmes will make use of subtitles throughout the programme; the usefulness of these is a matter for personal professional reflection. For independent learners they can be very supportive in decoding a prolonged text; on the other hand, they can convert the whole viewing experience into a reading task, which is probably not the main objective. It is odd how compulsive the reading of subtitles can become, even to people who can cope perfectly well with the language they are hearing!

Finally reading can be purposefully linked to the programme resource through the provision of some form of transcript. This can be used:

- to prepare the learners for what they are to view;
- to consolidate the language after the viewing;
- to provide focused learning activity.

USING TRANSCRIPTS

The transcript can be treated in particular ways in order to provide a range of activities:

- it can be used in the same ways as any reading text, and used either in advance or to follow up;
- it can be provided straight, in order for learners to follow what they hear;
- it can be used as a script for speaking work, either before or after the viewing;
- it can be broken up into sections, for which learners will provide titles or headings according to what they see on screen;
- sections can be rearranged in order for the learners to focus on the correct sequences;
- it can be gapped for individual words, in order for learners to fill the gaps;
- it can be gapped for whole phrases or sentences in order to focus attention on, for example, the replies to particular questions;
- details can be altered slightly to encourage learners to check for accuracy.

Finally, of course, the process can be reversed so that the learners are charged with producing the transcript of a programme clip in **writing**. This may be for purposes of checking comprehension and linguistic accuracy after the viewing, so that the challenge will be to recall as much of the scene as possible.

Alternatively the task may be to invent the dialogue *before* the listening activity. In this case, the learner views the sequence (e.g. a transaction in a shop) with no sound and then individually or as part of a group brainstorm, constructs an imaginary transcript for the scene. Here, the challenge is in the creative use of language the learner has largely already acquired, and the accuracy of the transcript in the light of the subsequent viewing is less important than the productive rendition of a possible solution to the problem.

Chapter 4
What's On?

DIFFERENT SORTS OF PROGRAMME

Different genres of programme are put together by their producers in distinctive ways and with a language content and idiom appropriate to the nature of the programme; the concision of a television advertisement, for instance, requires a completely different style and selection of language from those required by an extended documentary.

Programmes from educational and from mainstream broadcasting can therefore provide their own individual challenges and stimulus for linguistic activities, both in terms of their language and cultural content and in terms of their format, their style and the people they include. The fact that they are devised with different audiences in mind can be reflected in what we do with them in the classroom, and lead to considerations of the variety of lexis, grammar and register which learners can deploy.

It is important to consider what the potential is for each sort of programme on its own merits. An authentic information-based programme will provide much scope for identification of key words, specific vocabulary, detail or gist, and so invite particular sorts of language learning activities to exploit this. It would not seem sensible or productive, however, to use something like a soap opera, gameshow or entertainment show in the same way or for the same purpose, as the discourses and language involved as well as the viewers' affective response are quite different. The response anticipated by the programme's producer moulds the shape and appearance of the programme and will affect the teacher's exploitation strategies also.

WHAT TYPES OF PROGRAMMES ARE THERE?

Mainstream programmes available on satellite or cable may include:

- News and current affairs
- Interviews and chat shows
- Weather reports
- Sports
- Comedy

- Drama including soap opera
- Music
- Cartoons
- Advertisements
- Announcements
- Magazines and 'method' programmes
- Light entertainment and gameshows

All of these offer their own potential for language activities. Similarly, the existence of teletext, the continuing development of website resources (with text, sound and images) on the Internet and other digital technologies such as Data Broadcast open up yet further possibilities.

Key issues in evaluating the usefulness of such mainstream programmes and resources may include:

- the appropriateness of their theme;
- the general language level;
- the relevance of the programme;
- the length of individual segments within a programme;
- the pace of speech;
- the entertainment value.

These are all issues which resources planned specifically for education should make explicit, but which teachers evaluating authentic resources will need to look at for themselves.

Many modern educational programmes emulate some of the above formats purposely in order to capitalise on the motivational aspects of the television medium. They frequently include, for instance, vox pop interviews with 'real' people (i.e. not actors) or songs or animations. However they may also include their own unique features, such as:

- model situations;
- vignettes;
- examples of functional language in relevant situations;
- themed resources on specific issues, linked, for example, to examination syllabuses.

Some of the mainstream programme strands listed above can be broken down into smaller elements, each of which should be examined to see what they can offer the language classroom, firstly in terms of **linguistic content** which may be relevant at a variety of levels. This will help in identifying the type of authentic programme which may well be worth the time and effort of in-depth evaluation.

For example at a high level a sports programme may offer linguistic opportunities to give background information, talk about previous events, provide a commentary in writing or speech, compare performances or offer opinions on players.

At a much more basic level of language the programme may offer:

- illustrated portraits of some individuals or teams of interest to the learners (potentially including language of personal description, family life, interests, narrative in the past tense);
- a section with scores (including much practice of basic numbers, which can be used for listening acuity or for speaking work if the scores appear on screen as a list; likewise the ever-popular game of predicting the scores on the teleprinter from the presenter's intonation);
- teams in kit (stimulus for work on colours);
- a narrative (with language items which can be put into correct order);
- graphical presentations to stimulate speaking.

If, for the teacher, there seems to be scope within a programme for language work, the questions remain: *Will the class like to watch it?* and if so: *What can I get out of it?*

Possibilities for stimulating activities often reach well beyond the basic comprehension of language items within a clear context and should build on the intrinsic motivational content of the resource.

The programme may well have more stimulus to offer than good examples of the target language; it may also be interesting in terms of **genuine interactive potential**. For example certain groups of learners will, in real life, be interested in viewing a sports programme and want to talk about what is happening on the sports field. Viewing an extract from a game of football (for some people) can create genuine need for the production of certain utterances (praise, opinion, criticism, exclamations, questions, descriptions, prediction ...) which the teacher can adapt and build into the teaching scheme at a level relevant to the learners.

A potential sequence might be:

- Teacher presents language of opinions in one context.
- Class views part of a match and tries to use the learnt language.
- New language needs are identified by the teacher or requested by the learners.
- Teacher follows this up with further presentation.

This use of a resource with the potential for stimulating a real desire to say something opens up the possibility of imbuing the language itself with some personal significance for the learner.

Similar issues of personal interest will, of course, apply equally to other sorts of programmes for individual viewers, and the potential for activating adverse comments and criticisms by viewing a short clip should also not be ignored!

The next step after identifying potential interest of a particular programme is then to consider what sorts of learning activity may match up with the resource appropriately. These can include language practice activities, comprehension-based activities, and productive activities in writing and speaking. Often an individual programme resource will suggest a very specific and unique linked activity which emerges from the teacher's knowledge of her class, her own style and the essence of the resource itself.

The following list suggests a few generic areas of language activity related to the main types of programme resource, as a starting point. Some of the activities apply to more than one category:

Type of resource	Potential usefulness
News report	Matching Locating key words from context (e.g. job titles) Rebuilding a story from key words Inventing questions Comparing with a written text (e.g. a parallel newspaper article in the foreign or first language)
TV interview	Predicting questions Predicting answers Noting sense of questions Extending the interview Transposing to a written report Practice with reported speech Practice with the third person
Weather report	Interpreting key words Predicting words from the images Using the (silent) visuals to stimulate longer speech Transposing to a written digest

Sports	Listening focus on e.g. numbers Prediction e.g. of results on the teleprinter Reinforcing colours of team uniforms Providing a commentary
Comedy	Listening to intonation Describing people (physical and personality description) Identifying key words (e.g. in punchlines)
Drama	Using the transcript/script for oral performance Describing characters Making a transcript of a scene Writing a new scene Recounting what happened previously
Music show	Expressing personal tastes Electing a favourite song à la Eurovision Song Contest Identifying styles of music, drawing cultural parallels
Cartoon	Writing speech-bubbles Making a storyboard Making a new storyboard Drama roleplay
Advertisements	Identifying products Reproducing the voicetrack with appropriate intonation Identifying persuasive language (e.g. adjectives) Adapting the format for a new product
Announcements	Listening focus on times, titles, genres of programmes
Magazines and 'method' programmes (e.g. cookery)	Putting language into sequence Noting quantities, significant vocabulary Practice with imperatives Practice with recounting in the past tense Producing a different recipe
Gameshow	Replicating a section in roleplay Joining in with participative/predictive games Predicting the outcomes Commenting on people Offering advice Comparing with other games

There are some crucial differences between the educational effectiveness of purpose-made, as opposed to authentic resources. Whereas purpose-made resources will offer visual support linked to the language level of the proposed audience, in order to support comprehension, authentic programmes will not need to consider such detailed visual support, and may indeed wish to do something very different. Although the titles of, for example, a news programme usually fulfil a purely illustrative role, at times the images involved in an authentic programme are there as visual complements or contrasts to the words, so that the message takes a more analytical intellectual interpretation. For instance a political broadcast may be underscored by images of something showing a contrasting point of view, precisely to challenge rather than to support a literal interpretation, or to offer an ironical angle.

This sort of editorial issue may well be relevant to learners who are media-literate, of high ability or more mature, as for some students the deconstruction of this complex message may be a valid language task. However, it seems unlikely that interpreting such subtle messages would be a possible or relevant language activity for groups of lower ability or with less language experience.

Similarly, authentic programmes will not need to consider in their production the pace or range of the language used, although they will provide excellent examples of real language in use including a range of accents and dialects, of discourses and maybe lots of interruptions, fillers, hesitations, opinions, different exchanges etc. (depending on whether the programme is scripted or taken from life). Again, this may have particular relevance to some groups of learners (in the business area, for instance) but be entirely inaccessible to others. The best educational resources should identify and be clearly linked to a particular language level.

All of the above have particular implications for what sort of authentic programme resources a teacher may select for a particular class, but undoubtedly the biggest issue for teachers wishing to import such authentic resources obtained from satellite or cable or other means must be, once more, that of **time**:

- Time to find out what's on.
- Time to record the resources.
- Time to view the resources.
- Time to evaluate and fit them into the scheme of work.
- Time to plan the accompanying activities.
- Time to review the lesson subsequently.

As the value of authentic resources is very often to be found in their topicality, they do tend to have a brief lifespan, which makes the time issue even more constrained.

A system of collaborative planning between colleagues will help to spread the load of identifying useful and interesting broadcast resources, and with experience teachers will gain an overview of which programmes are likely to be the most relevant to their needs; however, a certain amount of enthusiastic commitment is required in this area!

It will be important to consider not only the general interest of the programme resource, but also how it fits in with the resources already to hand and in use, and how such resources will complement each other. For advanced learners, for instance, a task which requires them to contrast a television news report with a newspaper article on the same topic will be challenging and relevant.

The following format (reproduced in Chapter 8 on page 79 with a worked example) may help to focus the mind:

For authentic resources

Title: Source:

Date:

Type of programme: *News*   *Gameshow*   *Drama Animation*

                                     Advert   *Documentary*   etc.

Main subject:

Useful content:

Core language:

Age relevance:

Linked activities:

Linked resources:

Some specific genres of programmes offer particular ranges of practice and production activities. These are discussed in detail in Chapter 7, but some initial questions to support creative planning might be:

Q: *What is distinctive about this style of programme?*
       What are the implications? What possibility might this open up?

Strategies for productive use of different genres of authentic programmes often emerge from collaborative planning with colleagues. These
questions may provide a useful structure, e.g.:

> **Q:** *What is distinctive about <u>the production of a drama programme</u>?*
>
> **A:** *It is often based on a script which the actors need to rehearse, in order to
> establish sense, mood, appropriate intonation, etc. for the performance.*
>
> **Q:** *What are the implications?*

Four implications

(1) There could be scope in the language classroom for exploiting the
nature of 'rehearsal' in terms of 'drill'.
(2) Skills of appropriate intonation and pronunciation are sometimes
undervalued but can be equally as important as vocabulary and syntax.
This style of programme requires particular skills in these areas.
(3) 'Performance' is a central notion of the communicative approach to
language teaching. The concept of producing language 'for different
audiences' also comes in here. This must have potential.
(4) The existence of a script opens up opportunities for making clear links
between the written and spoken word.

> **Q:** *Songs are a popular ingredient of some programmes. Are they useful?*
>
> **A:** *Songs are made for repetition and participation. They aim to be instantly
> memorable to the listener.*

Four implications

(1) Learners may well internalise some of the language simply through
exposure to songs. Careful selection can contribute to their language
development and memorisation strategies.
(2) For some groups of learners involvement in the learning and performance of songs can be highly motivating.
(3) The regular rhythm (and sometimes rhyme-scheme) of a song can
support learners doing gapfilling activities for the real purpose of
obtaining a full version of the song text.
(4) As each song often has a readily identifiable and repetitive structure,
the possibilities for creative extension by the learners are considerable.

Using songs

Again there are great differences between using authentic songs, with their wide-ranging language and themes and their profound cultural significance, as opposed to purpose-designed songs, but, in either case the teacher will probably identify a linguistic feature of interest and devise a sequence such as this:

(1) **Setting the context.** Integrating visuals or key words related to the song text is useful to ease the way in.
(2) **Initial rehearsal of chosen language feature.** An activity which encourages the learners to use the language in e.g. a roleplay or Information Gap activity will heighten response to the same item when it occurs within the song.
(3) **Aural discrimination.** For the first listening the class may simply indicate when they hear the selected item(s).
(4) **Hearing the item embedded.** For the second hearing the pause feature may be used to extract a longer piece of language containing the chosen feature, check on meaning and rehearse its pronunciation.
(5) **Producing the item.** Once familiarity is established the sound control can be used to turn down the volume at key points to allow the class (or individuals) to say (or sing) the missing words. Alternatively a karaoke text can be produced or completed in writing. Public performance or recording may be a motivating activity for some groups of learners, but this needs to be handled sensitively, of course!
(5) **Building on the song structure.** In this final phase, the rhythm, line-length and even possibly rhyme scheme of the original song can be used by the learners to create their own similar text.

Finally, although this book focuses on the use of video, mention should be made of the ever-growing resources available to individual learners, and to establishments, through **on-line** means. The nature of this provision is:

- that digital broadcast technology offers the potential for extra resources alongside a programme (e.g. foreign language subtitles);
- that global information is available very rapidly via the computer-screen;
- that foreign language resources are available, although English tends to predominate internationally;
- that interactivity with this information is increasingly possible;
- that users can communicate with people at huge distances instantaneously, both in writing, through video-conferencing, whiteboarding and virtual encounters;

- that the information is available not only as text, but also as sound, images or moving images;
- that increasingly broadcast and computer technologies are converging so that viewers will be able to get access to moving video resources with high quality sound in an environment where they can manipulate it, discuss it and even edit it at the their own desktop.

As the technologies of telecommunications, broadcasting, and information technology draw closer together more sources of stimulus will be provided and consequently more language opportunities will be created. However, what is essentially the individual nature of the on-line experience at the moment will have implications for the sort of learning and research activities we devise, as purposeful human interaction will remain of the essence in the language-learning process.

Chapter 5
Tuning In

USING A MIX OF RESOURCES

Integrating new resources and approaches into the classroom is always a matter of some complexity for the teacher and the learners. In many cases a certain routine or rhythm of working has been established over a period of time, in order to provide reassurance and give people confidence that they know what to expect. The consistent use of a standard textbook, for example, can provide security, in that everyone knows what sort of sequence to anticipate.

However, sometimes this comfortable situation needs some change or challenge, either to motivate some types of learners, who need more variety or specific types of input, or indeed also to provide the teacher with something new and different to think about! Similarly, for learners working on their own at home, the introduction of a different sort of stimulus can enhance their learning experience and take them on to new discoveries about the process of language-learning.

The sort of input chosen may take the form of a resource (e.g. a text of a different sort, such as a video) or of an activity (i.e. what the learner does in response to the text). The very newness of certain resources or approaches can spark off new reactions in a class, but can also create some initial confusion or indeed some resistance to change. It is therefore important that **the teacher** be completely ready to import something different, be confident about what the resource is and how the lesson will work, and be persuaded that what they are about to do is really useful.

It is helpful if **the class** is prepared, in general, to accept that a variety of stimuli and activities will be used in order to provide many multisensory opportunities for them to learn about how best they learn themselves. Open-mindedness is a very desirable commodity!

The teacher's plans for incorporating a video resource will then be influenced by the extent to which the resource fits into her scheme of work, fits into her customary practice and fits in with what she knows of the needs and responses of a particular class.

In order to record (and share with colleagues) what contribution a particular resource may make to the experiences you wish to provide, an evaluation record sheet, as described above, may be useful. For the purposes of your own lesson plans for a particular week, the following format suggests things to take into account (a photocopiable version of this is included in Chapter 8, on page 80).

Memo worksheet for inclusion in scheme of work

Title of extract or programme:

Name of tape (if different):

Date needed:

Is tape available/booked:

Is the start of the extract easy to find?:

Equipment needed:

Is it available/operational/booked?:

Room needed:

Any particular requirements for the room?:

Other resources needed:

Worked example

Title of extract or programme:	*Clémentine Programme 5*
Name of tape (if different):	*Clémentine 1–10, BBC*
Date needed:	*Thursday*
Is tape available/booked?:	*Yes, on booking out form**
Is the start of the extract easy to find?	*Need to wind forward the night before*
Equipment needed:	*Video, monitor, OHP*
Is it available/operational/booked?	*Yes, but check the handset**
Room needed:	*My classroom*
Any particular requirements for the room?	*Extension cable and sockets needed to plug in video, monitor, OHP. Blinds.**
Other resources needed:	*Photocopied worksheets*

* Who will do this administrative and technical checking? Can I delegate some of these tasks to members of the class?

Initially it is important to know what you expect out of using the resource, as this will determine how you present and use it. As discussed above, if the main aim of the viewing is *motivation* then it may well not be appropriate to think of comprehension-based or grammar-based follow-up, as this could detract from the enjoyment of watching the programme. Again, if *viewing for pleasure* is the aim, this may also have implications for how much of the programme is viewed at one time. It can, after all, be very demotivating for viewers to have their viewing interrupted by a series of questions from the teacher or by the end of the lesson. On the other hand, the teacher may feel that a particular class needs a clear and relevant focus activity to have in mind whilst viewing, in order to keep their attention.

If, however, the aim of the viewing is *language development* then a certain amount of interruption is inevitable as the teacher picks up on certain images or language items to which the class will respond or with which they will be drilled.

Similarly, if the aim is to test *listening accuracy* there will possibly be a written outcome from the viewing, based on a worksheet or observation schedule. The implication here is not only that there will be a need for pauses while the learners cope with their writing task, possibly as the programme is running, but also with the number of viewings they will need.

WORKSHEETS

A major concern with linking worksheets to the programme is that of diluting the viewer's attention. If the learners are given a worksheet before the viewing to complete during the viewing, their attention will continually be divided between the screen and the page with the consequence that neither may receive proper thought.

A second problem is that the completion of the worksheet becomes the predominant objective, and the learners concentrate on completing that task rather than on the stimulus itself.

A third issue is that published worksheets often have more than one activity per page, and some viewers can easily be confused about which bit they are supposed to be doing at what time; this sometimes results in their answering questions based on completely the wrong section of the programme, or purely on hypothesis.

Screen tip: Worksheets
Possibilities for more effective sequences might be:
- viewing the programme section throughout for general observation and information; then issuing the worksheet before the second viewing.
- presenting the worksheet before the viewing to highlight what it's about, and potentially brainstorm suggestions, but then putting the worksheets to one side during the viewing.

This issue of **preparation for viewing** is important in trying to assure an effective learner response to the early uses of television resources, and such preparation may well mean incorporating a whole range of other classroom resources into the teaching sequence. The purposes of this preparation may be:

- to activate a bank of the foreign language in order to increase the likelihood of comprehension;
- to drill some feature of the language in order to speed up the process of viewing;
- to present particular unfamiliar items of the foreign language which are crucial for enjoyment or understanding of the clip;
- to rehearse a body of language connected with a particular language task (e.g. the language of giving opinions if the task is to review an aspect of the programme clip).

Preparation for viewing may take various forms:

- Stating the topic of the programme may be sufficient for able learners or those who have recently covered that topic in depth.
- This can lead into asking what language the learners already know connected with the identified topic and extending this language appropriately.
- Stating the main contents of the programme may provide sufficient context for some learners to be confident about finding their way through it.
- Presenting core vocabulary or structures may be essential for some learners to put them into the right frame of mind. Such presentation may well be by methods which are already familiar to the class, and involve visuals on flashcards or overhead projector transparencies, or written notes, or question and answer routines or reference to books.

The question '*How much language do I need to present first?*' will depend not only on the text itself but more importantly on the task to be set and the required outcome. An authentic resource concerning, for instance, a fashion show will undoubtedly contain a wide-ranging linguistic content, but this may not be so significant if the task set has as its focus the comprehension of, for example, the prices mentioned or the materials used. In other words the text is no more difficult than the task assigned to it.

If the level or pace of the language is too high for a particular group a task could, of course, still be devised, based solely on the visual aspects of the programme, e.g. to do with the colours seen or the viewers' own opinions of the garments. The listening element of the experience then becomes much more focused on listening to accent and intonation than listening to meaning.

LESSON REVIEW

Consideration of the preparatory phase of the lesson leads us also to think about the whole shape of that lesson and how the viewing fits into it.

At what point in the lesson does it come? If right at the start this can be problematical with pupils who will not want to do something more 'traditional' afterwards. If right at the end there is always the risk of interruptions and running out of time, or not being able to follow something up fully. In this position it can also seem rather like an add-on activity, whereas ideally the viewing will be integrated into the whole sequence of the lesson.

How much time is needed for the introduction and follow-up will, of course, depend on the individual lesson plan and the individual class, but in the early stages of experimenting with using the video the teacher is advised to maintain tight control over the time and record whether the preparation time allowed was sufficient and whether the follow-up or spin-off from the viewing should really have been allowed to run on longer than planned, in order to make the process more successful next time around.

A review document may help. A photocopiable version of such a document is included in Chapter 8, on page 81, and a worked example is shown on page 47.

Worked example: Lesson review

Class:	*14–15 years old*
Length of lesson:	*70 minutes*
Video resource used:	*Clémentine Programme 5*

Preparation phase

Other resources used:	*OHTs to talk about recent films*
Time allocated:	*10 minutes*
Was this sufficient?	*Only just; revision of the past tense needs more drilling*

Viewing phase

Time allocated:	*20 minutes played without pauses*
Pauses or repeats needed?	*Yes; we'll need to watch it again with pauses for consolidation; allow an extra 10 minutes in future*

Follow-up phase

Nature of follow-up:	*(a) Dialogue work – making a date, including writing* *(b) Vocabulary notes* *(c) Worksheet on past tense*
Time allocated:	*(a) 15 minutes. (b) 10 minutes (c) 15 minutes*
Was this sufficient?	*(a) Just about. (b) Yes. (c) Not yet marked!*
Other potential follow-up?	*Could try extended writing: a letter or narrative or the next scene of the story.* *Should try to link this up with an extended reading text.*

DEPARTMENTAL PLANNING

Where a teacher is working within a teaching department with an agreed syllabus or scheme of work it will be essential that the incorporation of a video resource contributes effectively to the aims of the department and to a particular teaching goal. It may be that, following trial with several colleagues within the department, the video resource and its concomitant activity actually delivers the required outcomes more effectively than the original resource (e.g. a course book). In this case the scheme of work will need to be amended to reflect this. The video resource will consequently replace, rather than supplement, the relevant section of the existing plan.

Video resources will not be most effective in isolation; other materials will enhance the viewing experience and extend the usefulness of the language into productive work. All of the familiar classroom resources will be valuable in preparing or following up the viewing:

- posters
- realia
- flashcards
- books
- OHTs
- playing cards
- worksheets
- props
- the video camera which enables prompt recycling
- the perimeter audio system which permits in-depth listening
- the black or whiteboard
- ICT.

Word processing, e-mail and video-conferencing will be increasingly useful for language work, as the means of delivering resources brings closer together the screen of the 'TV' and that of the computer. Such developments increase greatly the potential for learners at great distance from each other to share resources and discuss them with genuine feeling.

These resources can be invaluable in all stages of exploiting the resource and developing the language use:

Preparation

- presenting core language
- drilling
- presenting a key phrase to help them through
- brainstorming the topic
- looking at related pictures or text

Interaction

- repetition
- supporting comprehension or interpretation
- note-taking
- focusing attention for questions

Follow up

- rebuilding, using e.g. picture or word cues to build up or recap a dialogue

- discussion
- personalisation
- survey work
- transfer of language, e.g. from one situation to another.

Equally, classroom display can, of course, be linked beforehand to the theme or language of programme or can emerge from the programme to take work forward and be the focus for follow-up activity.

Chapter 6
Changing Channels

PRACTICAL MATTERS

As with any resource-based approach the management and care of video resources is crucial. Teachers planning to use a particular programme or programme section with a specific class on a certain day need to be confident that, on that day, they or their designated person will be able to:

- find the tape they need straight away;
- find the tape in usable condition;
- find the spot on the tape they wish to use;
- find the equipment ready to use;
- organise the classroom efficiently and quickly.

Additionally learners operating within a flexible learning environment or working by themselves at home need specific guidance in the handling of resources and equipment.

Within the classroom, confidence is often a crucial element in maintaining relationships and the working ethos; anything which compromises the confidence of either teacher or learners is consequently to be avoided. It follows that physical and other pragmatic management considerations are of the essence in preparing to use a programme resource, as the possibilities for classroom confusion and loss of teacher confidence are maximised as soon as there is technology involved!

It only takes one element of the panoply not to be in its expected place or one piece of hardware to go wrong and the fastidiously planned lesson can swiftly degenerate into awkwardness and embarrassment. For this reason it is often helpful to put in place a system for managing the various elements necessary to the smooth running of the lesson which involves other reliable people taking responsibility for certain arrangements. This, in principle, allows the teacher to focus primarily on the lesson organisation; in practice it is as well for the teacher to check that all is it should be anyway, and to have a backup plan for the lesson, just in case ...

The following are some of the practical considerations which a certain amount of planning and organisation can help with:

Tape management

Finding the tape   *Especially in a shared resource area*

Finding the spot on the tape   *Especially if it contains more than one item*

Maintaining the tape in a playable condition

Equipment management

Checking the equipment is   *Especially if it is shared or used for self-*
ready to use   *access*

Lesson management

Organising the classroom

Organising the activity

TAPE MANAGEMENT

Ideally, each teacher in a department will have their own copy of the video resources they intend to use, and will manage their own access and retrieval system. However, it will still be helpful if the system is shared, in case of emergency loans or exchanges and for shared reviewing purposes. If a department uses a shared scheme of work, it will clearly be desirable to have a common bank of 'approved' resources also.

In the more frequent situation where a central resources area is shared by a number of teachers it becomes highly desirable, if not essential, to have an easy, reliable and common system of cataloguing, referencing, maintaining and using the resources.

When an individual teacher finds a resource she/he likes to use with a particular age-group or topic it is fairly straightforward to plan that into the lesson plan and the long-term scheme of work and to place it appropriately in the resource area. Once the resource becomes shared by a department or a number of physically similar resources are around, however the potential for confusion becomes geometrically greater and greater.

In the case of videotapes the opportunities for things to go wrong are considerable. Here are just eight:

(1) all of the tapes in their 'naked' form look the same;
(2) a tape may contain more than one programme;

(3) a tape may not always be rewound;

(4) a tape may have been (wittingly or unwittingly) reused and over-recorded;

(5) a tape may have been replaced in the wrong sleeve;

(6) a tape may have been replaced damaged;

(7) a tape may have been copied and the copy replaced instead of the original; this will often produce a lower quality image and soundtrack upon replay;

(8) a tape may have been removed with no indication of its current whereabouts.

Recommendations may be as follows:

Problem	Recommendation
(1) You can't distinguish between tapes.	Stick the adhesive labels provided on to the cassette to indicate exactly what is on the tape.
(2) You have to wind and rewind through a lot of material.	Use shorter tapes and record only one programme per tape. Alternatively, use temporary self-adhesive labels to record at what point the tape has been left. The tape-counter may be useful here also.
(3) You can't tell immediately at what point the tape is.	Agree always to rewind the tape. Or use sticky labels as above to mark the current spot.
(4) The programme has been over-recorded.	Remove the tabs from the original video cassette to prevent over-recording.
(5) You find the wrong tape in the sleeve.	Use the extra labels provided to mark the tape sleeve in the same way as the tape itself.
(6) The tape will not play properly.	Have a system of identifying faulty or damaged tapes quickly. Have a back-up copy of the resources.
(7) The quality of the tape is less good than anticipated.	Use a colour-coding scheme on the labels so that the classroom version is always labelled in an agreed distinctive colour.
(8) You have to ask everyone if they have the tape.	Have a signing out system. For emergencies, use the back-up copy.

A cataloguing sheet for departmental use is included in Chapter 8 on page 82.

Annotated **cataloguing sheet for departmental records:**

Title:	*For quick reference.*
Videotape number:	*Useful if you have a lot of tapes.*
Tape length:	*Useful to speed up searching through.*
Recording date:	*Old tapes may need to be replaced some time.*
Contents:	*Titles of programmes/series on the tape.*
Notes:	*Are there confusing adverts or incidental programme clips between the main resources? Is a fragment of a programme missing? Is there anything to note about quality of picture or sound?*
Status:	*Is it the master copy?*

The back-up or reference version of a programme tape may be the original recording taken off-air, and may contain more than one programme per tape. This may be the master version used for making copies on to shorter tapes for classroom use, if you are licensed to make such copies. The quality of these copies is likely to be slightly inferior to the original, and any copies of this copy will increasingly become degraded. The best quality for reproduction is almost always that taken from broadcast itself.

Screen tips

Blank tapes are available in various lengths, from a few minutes only to several hours; for copying purposes the shorter the tape the easier it will be to locate the spot when required. Long tapes are useful for storing the whole of a series or a themed selection of clips; however, if damage occurs to a long tape this clearly means that you lose a great amount of material in one go.

If you record programmes on one system for playing on another, check that the two are compatible. For instance, a programme recorded at home on a double-speed recorder in order to save tape may well not be comprehensible at all on the single-speed player in the classroom!

The right for educational institutions to record broadcasts for educational uses and to make copies of recordings is often administered by an agency (in the UK the Educational Recording Agency) which issues licences.

The situation regarding published videotapes is entirely different, and is governed by the usual copyright laws; as it is not normally permissible to make copies of these, multiple copies may need to be purchased. However, some publishers offer beneficial licensing arrangements upon request.

Screen tips

Modern publications on videotape tend to be available in international formats; it is still important however to check that you order the format appropriate for your equipment. A common problem is that a tape from one system (e.g. SECAM) will only play in black and white on a player of another system (e.g. PAL).

Modern video players tend to use the VHS format of videotapes; some old machines and tapes were made in a format called Beta. The tapes are an entirely different shape, and are not compatible.

When planning to use a tape in a lesson, it is always advisable to check it before arrival in the classroom, to avoid embarrassment and losing time.

The tape itself

Not all tapes are identical, but the diagrams opposite illustrate some common features. In Figure 1 the window (a) allows you to see the rough position and length of the tape, which plays from left to right. This tape is at the start, and the transparent leader tape (e) is visible. The arrow (b) conveniently indicates which way to put the tape into the player! The tab (c) can be removed to prevent further recording on this tape. The closed edge (d) can be used for easily identified labelling, as it remains visible when the tape is put into its sleeve.

Figure 2 is seen from the opposite side and the button (f) is useful for opening the tape-flap as described below.

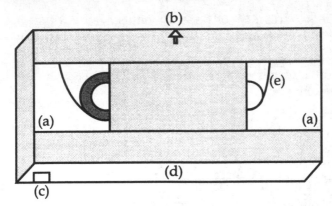

Figure 1

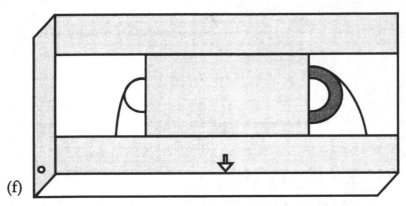

Figure 2

Beware tapes that rattle!

Faulty tapes can be very dangerous. If the tape becomes jammed it risks snapping, which will potentially lose a great deal of carefully prepared material; moreover, a jammed tape can cause damage to the video player's motor. Once a tape begins to act strangely (sticking, jumping, giving poor quality sound or pictures, or rattling) it should be checked. With a VHS tape this can be done by releasing the tape-flap with the button shown on the diagram.

If the tape has become twisted it can be straightened, but may very well give a poorer performance subsequently; likewise if the tape has developed an irregular surface or is not perfectly flat its quality will degenerate. In both these cases it would be worth considering replacing the tape.

The labels and box for video cassettes are very helpful, if used systematically. An agreed and shared departmental labelling system may include reference to:

- title(s)
- language and level
- topic relevance
- age-relevance
- particular scenes or items of interest.

As mentioned above, master copies should be clearly marked, and, if necessary, should have their tabs removed, to avoid accidental over-recording. Both tape and box should be marked in the same way, in order to avoid misplacement, and tapes should be kept in a secure, dry environment.

EQUIPMENT MANAGEMENT

> **Screen tips: The hardware**
> Do not assume that the video equipment at school will work as your domestic arrangement does. There are lots of variants on the theme!
>
> Get to know your set-up in advance.

This **elementary checklist** aims to cover the basics of what to do before the class arrives:

- Check that you know where the electric point is.
- Check that there are sufficient electric points for all of your equipment, in case you are also using OHP or audio or IT. If not, locate a multi-socket extension lead.
- If the equipment is in lockable cupboards, check who has the keys.

- Check what you have to do for the screen to come on. NB. Some screens have a standby function which takes effect if the screen is not used for a certain time. Check that you know how to reactivate the screen if this happens.
- Check which channel (if any) you need to select on the screen in order to view the video.
- Check what you have to do for the player also to come on.

- Check that the remote handset works, if there is one. It is a valuable tool to have to hand, as it liberates the teacher to move around the room, and keep eye contact with the class more easily than a control panel does. If there are two handsets, check which one operates the screen and which the player. In case the handset(s) cease(s) to work, check also where the fixed controls are on the screen and on the video player.
- Locate the 'eject' control, which is sometimes near the on/off control, and can lead to confusion!

- It may be useful to note the counter number (or the time counter) on the video player, in order to relocate the starting position efficiently later on.
- Check that your tape is at the right spot and that the controls work easily by playing a short section, pausing, stopping, playing on and rewinding.
- It is also useful to check the picture quality, colour and tracking at this stage. If you need to adjust things, it is worth making a mental note, as, when you switch the machine off, it may reset itself to its original position.
- Check the volume needed by moving around the room, but be prepared for adjustments; the character of the volume is likely to change when the room is full of people.
- Check visibility of the screen at the same time.
- Check that you can find the tracking and volume controls for the screen in case of the need for later adjustments.

- Checking the operation of the 'stop', 'pause' and 'play' controls is particularly important if you are planning to interrupt the viewing for one reason or another. If you press 'Stop' it is often the case that the tape will not restart at exactly the spot you stopped it at; the movement of the magnetic head on to the tape may leave a slight gap, omitting, maybe, a part of a word. When the 'stop' control is used on some machines, the tape is automatically rewound by a few seconds to ensure that no information is lost in this interruption. As this sort of very brief repetition of a section of language may well have value in reinforcing anyway, it may be worth considering doing this momentary rewind in any case, so that the sequence is:

> Pause/Stop   Very brief rewind   Play.

Using the 'pause' control may be more straightforward as the image on screen is still there to allow rewinding to an appropriate spot.

- Another foible of the 'pause' control is worth checking on also, especially if you are planning an extended interruption to the viewing. In many cases the pause function is set to switch itself off after a certain time, in order to save wear on the tape and the motor, so that the player will suddenly either begin to play the tape again, seemingly of its own volition, or it will switch the tape off. This latter can be a distraction if the screen in use also doubles as a television, in which case the currently broadcast show may unexpectedly erupt on to the screen! In any case, protracted use of the pause button is bad practice, as it tends to risk stretching the tape.

- If the equipment is used by other people, they may need to change the configuration of the connecting cables (in order to view television rather than video, for instance.) It is advisable, therefore, to check how the connections between the video player and its monitor work so that such changes can be put right. As there are usually only a couple of cables involved, it is not too complex to make a diagram of which plug goes into which socket.

- If your equipment has a proper cabinet with doors, these can be adjusted to reduce the amount of reflection present on the screen.

Not all of these features apply to every machine of course, but it is worthwhile getting to know your equipment and how to solve frequent minor worries at the outset.

Screen tips: Trouble-shooting	
No picture on screen	Is the monitor switched on?
	Is it on standby?
	Is the tape in?
	Is it just the blank tape before the recording?
	Is the player on?
	Is it on 'pause'?
No/wrong picture	Is the monitor set for the video channel?
	Is it the right tape?
No sound	Is the mute button on?
Flickering picture	Is the tracking correct?

LESSON MANAGEMENT

Organising the classroom

In the background to the individual lesson is another level of planning to do with the whole of the teaching department or indeed of the whole institution. Considerations need to be made, for example, of the appropriateness of particular rooms for using audio-visual equipment.

Important features of the classroom

- access to sufficient power points;
- accessibility for the video trolley if needed;
- desirability of blinds, sound-proofing, carpet;
- undesirability of much direct sunlight;
- the size and shape of the room itself;
- seating arrangements which allow teacher–pupil eye contact during viewing;
- furniture which is appropriate to the lesson and the number of pupils in the class;
- visibility of the screen for learners; a raised screen is often desirable, but sometimes viewers need to read on-screen captioning.

If the television viewing area is not the teacher's usual teaching room other organisational factors come in to play. Any migration of students from their well-established paths can, of course, lead to their 'getting lost' on the way to the lesson, with the consequent effect on starting off properly and the extent of time available. Once they have arrived, the new or unusual surroundings or views from the windows may prove to be more fascinating than the prospect of work, with consequent effects on the attention span of the class.

In some cases the necessity of booking 'the television room' or indeed 'the television' can be the first and biggest impediment to a teacher's use of broadcast resources. If the departmentally shared hardware is generally stored in one particular room, it can be the case that the person attached to that room becomes proprietorial about the video trolley.

If the room is available to the whole school to book *ad hoc*, this procedure can sometimes involve protracted negotiations with the teacher who normally inhabits the allocated space, or with the technician whose fiefdom it may have become. If the designated room is within the department but used as a teaching space by someone else, plan to swap well in advance.

Anything which takes teachers and/or students out of their established routine risks being instantly destabilising. Hence, in an ideal situation, teachers would have ready access to the equipment they need within their own classroom, with proper security measures and access to technical support when needed. In the long term, departments which intend to make regular use of specific equipment may well wish to prioritise the purchase and maintenance of such equipment within its (and the institution's) development plan.

Organising the activity

The planning questions outlined in Chapter 3 will identify what sorts of resources are needed to introduce, supplement or extend the viewing activity. Other questions to ask may include:

- *Who does what?*
  Who gets the equipment ready or pulls the blinds?
- *What happens first?*
  It is important, of course, to settle the class and set up the work to be done.
- *What does the teacher do?*
  This question will lead to consideration of how the teacher progresses from simple playing of the tape to more confident use of the resource.
- *What does the teacher avoid doing?*
  It is, as always, important to remember the teacher's role in motivating the class. When watching a video resource, such motivation is immediately undermined if the teacher is not clearly viewing at the same time as the class. Speaking over the soundtrack of the programme is almost always counter-productive, as the class becomes confused and ends up either listening more intently to the tape or ignoring the tape to listen to the teacher, or indeed listening to neither.

Screen tips

Do

- be in a good position to view both class and screen
- show interest in the programme

Don't

- be in a position which obscures the view of the screen
- talk over the programme soundtrack

PROGRESSION IN THE RANGE OF ACTIVITIES

Part of the rationale for including programme resources in the scheme of things is to provide more variety in the range of stimulus available to language learners. Once the teacher has mastered the basics of the technology and introduced some teacher-centred, controlled activities successfully he or she will be ready to progress to more adventurous ideas, and thereby support the learners in developing more independent language-learning skills. The progressions may be:

- From **closed** to **open-ended** tasks.
  From *View and note the key information x, y and z* to *View and make notes*.

- From **single input** to **multiple stimulus** activity.
  From video + worksheet to video + OHP + flashcards + audio-cassette + roleplay, etc.

- From **reactive** to **proactive** tasks.
  From activities based on comprehension and reproduction of language to activities leading to original production.

- From **content-bound** to **experimental** tasks.
  From *View and recognise* to *Speculate*.

- From **prescriptive** tasks (appropriate to people learning by themselves) to **less-prescriptive** tasks.
  From *View and express your opinions* to *View and then prepare your own presentation*.

Students viewing alone clearly need a much tighter structure than a class being taught, whose viewing can be mediated. Lone learners will need to understand the purposes and intended outcomes of their viewing and will need to focus their attention on particular features if they are not to be swamped by the flow of the language and images. They should clearly understand what is to be gained by going through a productive sequence such as this:

Previewing   Getting a sense of the gist of the whole clip by 'fast forwarding' or viewing without soundtrack.

Brainstorming Raising listening expectations by thinking ahead to what language is likely to be used.

Isolating   Identifying the crucial language items or keywords of the clip by listening to it; writing these down can help subsequent reference work.

Rebuilding   Using the notes taken to restate the content of the clip.

Elaborating   Adding additional ideas or opinions.

Comparing   Introducing contrasting ideas, possibly from other sources of reading.

Structuring   Using the logical thread of the programme clip, with relevant adaptations, to structure a subsequent piece of writing or an oral presentation.

Two reminder sheets suggesting some strategies for independent learners are included in Chapter 8 on page 83.

In all of these practical concerns it is important that the teacher and viewers feel comfortable with the resource and with what is expected of them; this atmosphere of safety may well take some development on all sides in its own right. As the orchestrator of the learning experience the teacher will welcome the support and collaboration of colleagues in matters technical as well as pedagogical.

Chapter 7

Exploitation Strategies

VARIETY OF APPROACH

The contents and style of particular programmes suggest and allow for a variety of linked language activities. Likewise the mechanics of what the video player and monitor can do allow for certain combinations which teachers can exploit. Viewers can:

- watch and listen to the whole of a programme or sequence;
- watch a sequence with no sound;
- listen to a sequence with the visuals concealed;
- pause the tape at a particular image;
- rewind the tape to a particular point;
- rewind in order to re-play;
- fast forward the tape;
- or, of course, switch the whole thing off!

Each of these presents us with a variety of possibilities for language work, e.g.:

- extended viewing for pleasure;
- invention of an appropriate soundtrack;
- identification of context, relationships or mood;
- extension, questioning or description;
- text analysis;
- drill or rehearsal;
- identification of gist;
- discussion or incorporation of other linked resources.

It may be desirable, for instance, to combine the programme input with other learning resources by:

- using complementary visuals on flashcards or OHTs;
- having corresponding wordcards available;
- having transcripts available;
- having edited transcripts available;
- having gap-fill transcripts available;
- having worksheets available;
- having realia or props available.

Consolidation or preparation away from screen can be most effective when it builds on a variety of resources.

As the usefulness of particular technical strategies tends to emerge through practical experimentation, a recording sheet is included in the photocopiable Chapter 8 for teachers to make their own notes on techniques which have worked for particular purposes in particular cases (page 85).

Familiarity with the technical potential and the exact content of different programme resources leads to an enhanced and more creative view of the sort of use to which the programmes may be put to use with language learners. For the teacher in the early stages of using video resources in the classroom key planning issues will include:

- the teacher's own personality;
- the teacher's style of classroom management;
- the teacher's confidence in managing a range of resources;
- the teacher's styles of teaching and attitude to centralised and decentralised classroom activity.

Screen tips
Start by playing to your strengths and then develop new ones.

In consequence many learning activities may begin from a tightly-controlled scenario, where the teacher manages individual or whole class work, probably through a text-based activity and often with a focus on comprehension of the language content of the programme viewed.

Progressively the teacher can then try out more adventurous activities involving the class in speaking work, pairwork, groupwork, research, spontaneous response activity, productive creation or extended drama, as the case may be.

The worksheet

The caveat for starting with text-based worksheets and integrating them into the scheme of things must always be the practical one of how people will cope with them. If a learner is asked to:

- view a television resource including a foreign language soundtrack;
- read a worksheet or other piece of text;
- answer questions or fill in gaps;

all at the same time, the sensory overload and potential for confusion is clearly very great.

For this reason it is often more helpful to think of **sequencing** these items into stages which can be coped with, so that:

- firstly, the learners may simply view the programme sequence to get a flavour or the gist;
- secondly, they may see the text on the worksheet and have time to absorb it;
- thirdly, they may focus on the task associated with the text and use the programme to help them complete it.

They may still need to view the programme more than once, of course.

It often makes more sense to view the whole of the programme or sequence first, especially when working with product-minded learners (i.e. those whose main aim is to get the task completed, often male learners) as, once they see a worksheet, they become fixated on filling it in, and can often put all their energy into that, to the detriment of what they are actually expected to listen to or view.

Increasing confidence will gradually allow consideration of other possibilities for using a video-text, as well as 'listening and understanding'. Some such are outlined below.

What else to do with programmes?

Screen tips
It is useful to build up a variety of approaches.
It is essential to build on the strengths of the resource.
It is interesting for the students to be learning something else at the same time as encountering the language.

As well as for **Comprehension** programmes can provide stimulus for, among other things, **Personalisation**, **Comparison**, **Prediction**, **Hypothesis**, and **Repetition**.

The following sequence moves from tightly-controlled to more open-ended activities, and suggests what may be appropriate for whole class choral activities, individual work, pair work, group work, and other interactions. Some may be useful in several situations of course.

Comprehension: Activities with a tightly controlled focus relating to the spoken content of the programme

These can be varied according to the experience or expertise of the learners, maybe starting from activities which are simple to understand and require little linguistic production and then moving up the scale, e.g. True and false exercise; multiple choice exercise; gap-filling from a multiple choice; gap-filling from memory.

Whole class	Examples
Spotting keywords and responding	By raising hands or saying the word.
Physical response	Following instructions with props.
Brainstorming	In preparation for listening or to summarise.

Individual	Examples
True/false activities	*Is it mentioned?*
Sequencing	Numbering a list as things are mentioned or manipulating picture or word cards into a sequence.
Ticking activities	Filling a grid.
Answering questions	With or without multiple choice answers.
Note-taking without writing	Making a poster.
Note-taking (brief writing)	Making an identity card for a person.
Comparing the spoken text with a transcript	Reading and checking. Proofmarking a text.
Cloze activities	Gap-filling with or without a wordlist to help.
Matching	*Who said what?* Matching titles or descriptive words/ phrases with programme segments.

While pupils working independently have the partial advantage of being able to view, review and check their understanding under their own steam and with as much repetition as necessary, those working with other people have the opportunity to obtain appropriate guidance, motivation, challenge and feedback directly.

Pairwork	Examples
Marking grids and comparing with a partner	This can include coping with distractors.
Sequencing text	A disassembled selection of the transcript.
Text reconstruction	Rebuilding the soundtrack with the sound off, in writing.
Grouping	Collecting information about one person from several sections of the programme.

Group activities	Examples
Making collaborative lists	Sharing tasks to get a fuller picture.
Sorting	Allocating programme clips to categories.
Matching	Titles of clips to items in a programme.
Comparing	A TV news item with a printed one.
Brainstorming	Inventing titles for sections of a programme.
Recording	Making a written summary.
Translation and re-translation	
Asking questions	Creating 'true/false' or multiple choice tasks.

Other stimuli: Activities with a focus relating to the other features of the programme:

Whole class	Examples
Choral drilling	Rehearsing pronunciation.
Brainstorming	Re-constructing the text from key words or images.
Spoken gap-fill	Reconstructing the soundtrack of a tape when the volume is off, in speech.
Identifying keywords from the context	Picking politicians' job titles from a news report on a conference.

Individual	Examples
Personalising the text	Amending the version on screen to be personal.
Inventing a possible soundtrack	Creating a dialogue based on the pictures only.
Inventing an alternative soundtrack	Varying the core language to another context.
Inventing a humorous soundtrack	By changing the context or roles completely.
Identifying feelings and moods	
Transposing	From the spoken text to a written version.

Pair/Group	Examples
Discussion	*Who do you think is … happy/… in charge, etc.?*
Rehearsing a dialogue or a group scene	
Sequencing text based on the picture only	Using an edited transcript.
Devising a storyboard	
Creating questions	About the visual aspects of the programme.
Prediction	What someone will say, what will happen.
Making a résumé	

A reminder sheet **Potential Extension Activities** is included in the photocopiable Chapter 8 (page 84).

The stimulus for **Comparison** may have a language element as its primary objective, in order, for example, to develop a range of vocabulary around a particular topic by comparing what the presenters say with one another, or directly with the language learner (e.g. *He lives in a small flat in the middle of a city, but I live on a farm by a river*). Most frequently, however, there will also be an underlying cultural awareness involved in such comparison. This can provide stimulus for explicit discussion.

CULTURAL CONTENT

The cultural elements of a curriculum may focus on:

- providing access to authentic materials (e.g. real objects, letters, printed material, photographs, stories and anecdotes, film and video material);
- encountering native speakers of the chosen language;
- general knowledge about the target language countries (history, society);
- knowledge of particular cultural icons (famous places and people);
- awareness of behaviours and of social factors (terms of address, greetings);
- awareness of everyday life;
- awareness of multicultural issues;

in order to encourage positive attitudes to difference and to the language-learning process itself.

Many of these elements may naturally be present to one degree or another within documentary films made in a country where the language is spoken, but the teacher will need to consider what features of these elements are relevant to learners at particular stages, what should be made explicit at what points and to what extent this cultural dimension should be a spur to work within the foreign language.

Clearly, with young beginners, the aim will be to provide motivation and interest in the new language; chosen images may therefore feature very positive topics and illustrate what similarities there are between cultures in order to give reassurance that all is not strange! As such learners will not have sufficient competence in the new language (or possibly inclination) to be able to analyse cultural issues in depth for a certain time, activities need to be at an accessible level, and it is here that the visual aspect of a television resource comes into its own.

Screen tips:
Matching the cultural element to the linguistic sequence:
(1) Start from visual aspects (viz. below).
- Observe the extra-linguistic (social behaviours, body language and gesture) as well as the language itself.
- Focus on linguistic conventions.
(2) Ask for personal parallels and responses.
- Encourage questions.
(3) Encourage empathy.

Culture: A sequence using television resources

(1) **Observation**
- Learners observe someone talking about themselves and then personalise the language used. (They use 1st person verbs e.g. to describe their breakfast habits).
- Learners observe and identify features they know the target language word for.
- Learners ask about significant features they observe that interest them. The teacher presents relevant vocabulary or phrases in the target language.

(2) **Comparison**
- Learners observe real people in more or less natural situations. They devise questions to ask them and roleplay interviews including their (real or hypothesised) answers (2nd person verbs).
- They narrate what they discover about these people (3rd person verbs).
- They begin to make comparisons, identifying similarities as well as differences.

(3) **Extension**
- Learners use the knowledge they have acquired about the people and places observed to ask questions in the form of a quiz (Question forms).
- Learners use the structure of the presentations to create their own parallel presentation. For example they view a description of a small town square in the target language country and observe what is there (shops, other buildings, etc.). They then create a similar description of, e.g., the place where they live, highlighting the contrasts (Negative forms).
- Learners perform roleplays with reference to what they have observed.
- Learners begin to explore stereotypes.

In some areas, such as this cultural one, it may become evident to the teacher that the video resource can in fact a much richer stimulus than the stock item regularly used in the scheme of work, because it:
- is easily accessible
- is visually very clear
- is linguistically focused
- appeals to many groups of learners
- provokes interest
- leads to many outcomes.

It is at this point that the video becomes a primary resource, replacing, rather than supplementing, something which does the job less well.

ENGAGING CREATIVITY

One of the issues which may emerge from using a variety of teaching stimuli and teaching/learning strategies is that opportunities arise for a broader, more fluid and imaginative approach to language work. In particular the multisensory combination of images, words and music which coexist in a television programme can spark off many different lines of thought (and hence of language work) both in the teacher and in the minds of the learners. Such responses may involve the learners' real life skills, their memory, their powers of observation, their opinions, and their own sense of humour as well as their language knowledge and skills.

Hence, what may begin as an illustrated spoken text on screen can turn into the core of a much more creative process; the important attitudes for the teacher to maintain are her own open-mindedness to potential spin-off activities, an acceptance that such activities require time for thought and response and the class's awareness that their ideas, responses and elaborations are very welcome (especially if they come in the language being learnt).

As ever, some of the more effective follow-up activities will be carried out away from the television screen and will involve other resources, such as word-processing or recording hardware.

In sequence from closed to more open-ended activities the teacher's focusing questions may move from the concrete, text-linked:

What? *What is it? What has happened previously?*

Who? *Who is it? Who said it?*

When?

to the more analytical

How? *How does this happen?*

Why? *Why does X do/say that?*

to the more interpretative

What *is X like?*

What *do you think?*

to the more inventive

Now what?

and into the more critical or deconstructional approaches of media studies, or the more free-flowing area of creativity. A programme stimulus which is clearly not factual may open up the viewer's linguistic imagination.

Viewers of a fiction:

- focus on characters, incidents associated with them, catchphrases or descriptors. They use these to develop pen portraits, or devise multichoice or gap-filling activities, or for creating information forms or posters. Information can be gathered collaboratively by groups who then convert it into a cardgame.
- hypothesise about e.g. the other (unseen) side of a telephone conversation or what will happen in the next episode.
- use the résumé pictures at the start of an episode to recall events, offer views, practise talking about the past.
- use picture or word cues as prompts to rebuild a section of dialogue.
- sequence pictures or sections of text as a storyboard in order to direct a live performance.
- direct a group performing a scene using only the script and then comparing the outcome with that on-screen.
- view a scene with no sound in order to write a potential script; they subsequently perform their version in contrast with the original clip.
- extend the narrative, adding a new scene, making an alternative version or editing the script.
- create particular sorts of roleplay in the style of the character chosen, building on quirks or identifying features.
- invent interviews and ask questions of someone representing a character.
- rehearse dialogues from the story chorally by the class in sections, each section taking a different role for pronunciation practice; subsequently students can work individually or in pairs to generate similar, but different versions of the exchanges.

Viewers of any type of programme:

- replicate the structure of a clip, doing something similar relating to their own interests, imitating the format.
- transpose the text to a written account, or vice versa prepare a spoken report based on a text which they then compare with a programme clip.
- produce textual items in keeping with the programme item in question, e.g. possible publicity posters for a drama, newspaper billing, running order, magazine review.

Viewers of an advert:

- change the product, but retain the style of the TV advert, imitating the particular speech patterns.
- transpose the content of the advert into a written or printed form, selecting and editing the language accordingly.

More able/experienced learners

Students contrast a television report with a printed report on the same theme; they then summarise the articles, balance the arguments and add their own views in writing or in speech.

Students comment on the choice of background visuals, music, presenters, other talking heads or language in the light of their interpretation of the programme content. Groups could look at different aspects of the programme (e.g. what is actually said as opposed to what is seen) and what the subtext seems to be, in order to lead to a debate.

A note of caution in such analysis has to be that it can become rather dry and academic for some students. As ever, it is important to match appropriately *the learners, the resource* and *the chosen activity*.

Screen tips
Creativity using broadcast resources
Creative stimulus is available:
- for review (constructively criticising dramatic style, presentation or language)
- for performance '... in the style of ...'

Creative contexts are available as models:
- for performance (songs, rhyme, drama; media, gameshows)
- for game-playing, and for publication.

Readily available activities (in a sort of sequence):
- personalising, guessing, hypothesising (*'What if ...?'*)
- offering views, responding
- replacing or manipulating the language
- transposing, adapting, recombining, adding ideas
- elaborating, inventing.

In terms of using a drama, the following are examples of such a sequence:

- **Personalising**
  Using the (tran)script to rehearse language.
- **Guessing**
  Identifying unfamiliar words from the context.
- **Hypothesising**
  What if Z said xxxxxx?
- **Offering views**
  Do you like ...? What do you think of ...? Why do you think ...?

- **Responding**
  to characters; to events; to techniques.
- **Transposing**
  Converting a scene into a written script; producing a written description.
- **Adapting**
  Creating a role-play in the style of a character.
- **Adding ideas**
  'Who ...?' 'What do you think is happening?' 'Why ...?'
- **Elaborating**
  Introducing characters or events. The story so far ... 'What next ...?'
- **Inventing**
  Make up a new conversation (argument, teasing, explanation, berating, interview).
  Adding a scene.

The creative context of a television programme can, in summary open up the imagination and the critical and creative response of our language learners through and in the foreign language.

Chapter 8
Schedules and Checklists

The schedules and checklists on the following pages are intended to be used by teachers working independently or in departments. They can be photocopied and used to guide discussion or can be completed and inserted into a departmental scheme of work. As teachers become more familiar with the use of video resources these schedules can be amended for their particular needs.

Evaluation Schedule

General
Title of the programme/series:

Suggested target age:

Stimulus
Does it provide good and clear models for replication?

Does it allow for easy interruption for explanation, repetition or questioning?

Motivation
Will the overall design of this programme appeal to the target group of learners?

Is it an appropriate style or genre?

Does it provide a range of different speakers?

Are the people in the programme interesting?

Level
Does it fit with the maturity level of the teaching group?

Is the language level largely appropriate to the target group?

Quality
Are the examples of the target language relevant and clear?

Does the programme present good models of pronunciation and intonation?

Context
Do the visual elements help clarify the language appropriately through context clues?

Flexibility
Is the content of the programme relevant to the scheme of work and/or the learners' needs and interests?

Are the segments of the programme of the right length for this group?

Would sections of the programme interest other teaching groups?

Culture
Are the images supportive of developing cultural awareness?

Ease of use
Are the programme segments clearly labelled?

Other criteria

Worked Example of Evaluation Schedule

General
Title of the programme/series: *BBC Jeunes Francophones*

Suggested target age: *14-16*

Stimulus
Does it provide good and clear models for replication? *Yes.*

Does it allow for easy interruption for explanation, repetition or questioning?
Sections are clearly identifiable.

Motivation
Will the overall design of this programme appeal to the target group of learners?
Many of them.

Is it an appropriate style or genre? *Yes.*

Does it provide a range of different speakers? *Yes, in different contexts.*

Are the people in the programme interesting? *They are of the same age as the pupils.*

Level
Does it fit with the maturity level of the teaching group? *Yes. Topics are addressed in teenage style.*

Is the language level largely appropriate to the target group?
Fits largely with my examination syllabus (Some topics less so).

Quality
Are the examples of the target language relevant and clear? *Interesting accents.*

Does the programme present good models of pronunciation and intonation?

Context
Do the visual elements help clarify the language appropriately through context clues?
Often, yes.

Flexibility
Is the content of the programme relevant to the scheme of work and/or the learners' needs and interests? *Some topics fit very well with revision syllabus.*

Are the segments of the programme of the right length for this group?
Programmes are 20 minutes long, broken up into segments.

Would sections of the programme interest other teaching groups?
Francophonie issues relevant to older students.

Culture
Are the images supportive of developing cultural awareness?
Three French-speaking areas are featured.

Ease of use
Are the programme segments clearly labelled?
They are fairly consistent: documentary, voxpop interviews.

Other criteria

Planning Schedule

Teaching resource:

Why am I using it?

What do I want out of it?

Which bit do I use for this purpose?

What preparation will the class need?

What interaction will there be?

What follow-up will there be?

Worked Example of Planning Schedule: 1

Teaching resource:	*Gameshow*
Why am I using it?	*Personal identification language; questions in context.*
What do I want out of it?	*Creation of new dialogues.*
Which bit do I use for this purpose?	*Introduction mostly.*
What preparation will the class need?	*Brainstorm of core questions.*
What interaction will there be?	*On second viewing, pauses to repeat.*
What follow-up will there be?	*Groupwork to prepare a new scene.*

Worked Example of Planning Schedule: 2

Teaching resource:	*Ruck Zuck (RT2)*
Why am I using it?	*Personal identification language; stimulus for language development work*
What do I want out of it?	*(1) Set up communicative activity and (2) illustrate brainstorming.*
Which bit do I use for this purpose?	*(1) Chinese Whisper game (2) Wordgame (cf. Blankety Blank)*
What preparation will the class need?	*Very little*
What interaction will there be? .	*Encouraging enjoyment*
What follow-up will there be?	*We'll do the activity afterwards*
Dictionary work.	

Record Sheet for Evaluating Authentic Resources

Title:

Source:

Date:

Type of programme: News   Gameshow   Drama   Animation
                          Advert   Documentary etc.

Main subject:

Useful content:

Core language:

Age relevance:

Linked activities:

Linked resources:

Worked Example of Record Sheet

Title: *Questions pour un champion*   Source: *TV5*

Date: *Winter '97*

Type of programme: News   <u>Gameshow</u> Drama   Animation
                      Advert   Documentary etc.

Main subject: *Quiz game*

Useful content: *Cultural information*

Core language: *Personal identification*

Age relevance: *Older students (programme features adults)*

Linked activities: *Creating quiz questions in French for a team game*

Linked resources: *Reference books for quiz information*

Memo Record for Inclusion in Scheme of Work

Title of extract or programme:

Name of tape (if different):

Date needed:

Is tape available/booked:

Is the start of the extract easy to find?

Equipment needed:

Is it available/operational/booked?

Room needed:

Any particular requirements for the room?

Other resources needed:

NB. A worked example appears in Chapter 5

Lesson Review

Class:

Length of lesson:

Video resource used:

Preparation phase

Other resources used:

Time allocated:

Was this sufficient?

Viewing phase

Time allocated:

Pauses or Repeats needed?

Follow-up phase

Nature of follow-up:

Time allocated:

Was this sufficient?

Other potential follow-up?

NB. A worked example appears in Chapter 5

Cataloguing Sheet for Departmental Records

Title:

Videotape number:

Tape length:

Recording date:

Contents:

Notes:

Status:

Watching Alone: Reminder Sheet 1

Why are you listening/viewing?	Accordingly, what could you do?
For comprehension?	make a précis of a short clip
For intonation?	imitate
For pronunciation?	repeat
For vocabulary or idiom?	note words to look up
For fluency?	rephrase or reiterate
For information?	jot down notes

Watching Alone: Reminder Sheet 2

Listening Skills	Strategies
Raising expectations	Fast forward to check on contents. Brainstorm key language accordingly. Prepare yourself with a dictionary.
Gist comprehension	Identify the key sentence in a text (e.g. a potential title).
Detail comprehension	Identify key vocabulary.
Note-taking	Take bullet point notes. Summarise the item to a word limit.
Add personal opinions	
Self-expression	View; then replay and supply some of the language used.
Language development	Note the structuring words. Balance the arguments

Potential Language Extension Activities

Listening	Activities
Comprehension of key words	Question and answer
	Putting in order
	True/False
	Writing in target language
Comprehension of gist	Matching titles
	Writing a title
	Identifying words in transcript

Speaking	Activities
Pronunciation	Pausing and repeating
Intonation	Freezing and recalling
	Predicting
	Drilling
	Performing from script
Taking the initiative	Expressing opinions
	Performing from a silent cue
	Making contrasts
	Linking to other resources

Writing	Activities
Make notes	Selecting keywords to rebuild
	Selecting descriptive words
	Adding descriptive language from the pictures
	Writing an outline
Compare	Spotting cultural similiarities and differences
Transpose	Converting from 1st to 3rd person in context of a report
	Converting a script into a narrative
Questions	Writing questions about a scene
Extend	Adding a verse/a scene

Getting the Most from the Equipment

Strategies

1. Watch the whole of a sequence
Outcome

Example

2. Watch a sequence with no sound
Outcome

Example

3. Listen to a sequence with the visuals concealed
Outcome

Example

4. Pause the tape at a particular image
Outcome

Example

5. Rewind the tape to a particular point
Outcome

Example

6. Rewind in order to re-play
Outcome

Example

7. Fast forward the tape
Outcome

Example

References

Altman, Rick (1989) *The Video Connection: Integrating Video into Language Teaching*. Boston, MA: Houghton Miflin. ISBN 0395-481430.

Choat E. and Griffin, H (1986) Young children, television and learning. *Journal of Educational Television* 12 (2), 91–104.

Bates, A.W. (1981) *Some Unique Characteristics of Television and Some Implications for Teaching and Learning* (IET Paper on Broadcasting, No. 180). Milton Keynes: Open University, Institute of Educational Technology.

The Educational Recording Agency Ltd (ERA). 74 New Oxford Street, London WC1A 1EF.

Hawkins, Eric (1984) *Awareness of Language: An Introduction*. Cambridge: Cambridge University Press.

Richard Johnstone (1994) *Teaching Modern Languages at Primary School: Approaches and Implications* (Scottish Council for Research in Education Minipaper 14). Edinburgh. ISBN 0-947833-97-8.

Kozma, R.B. (1991) Learning with media. *Review of Educational Research* 61 (2), 179–211).

Mueller, Guenther A. (1980) Visual context clues and listening comprehension: An experiment. *Modern Language Journal* 64.

SCAA (1997) *Modern Foreign Languages in the National Curriculum: Managing the Programme of Study, Part 1: Learning and Using the Target Language. June, 1997*. SCAA publications are now available from the current UK National Curriculum body, QCA, 2a Bolton Street, London W1Y 7PD.

Sharp, Caroline (1995) *Viewing, Listening, Learning: The Use and Impact of Schools Broadcasts*. Slough: NFER. ISBN 0-7005-1373-6.

Programme examples

Clémentine. (1996) BBC Education, White City, 201 Wood Lane, London W12 7TS. Website: http://www.bbc.co.uk/education/

Jeunes Francophones. (1994) BBC Education, White City, 201 Wood Lane, London W12 7TS Website: http://www.bbc.co.uk/education/

Questions pour un champion. TV5. TV5 publishes regular brochures entitled *'Apprendre et ensigner avec TV5'* including strategies for using particular programmes and listings of current broadcasts. Website: http://www.tv5.org

Ruck Zuck. RT2.

German satellite TV as a source of teaching and learning materials. Paul Mohr lists and describes many satellite and terrestrial providers of broadcasts in *German Teaching* No. 15, June 1997 (Association for Language Learning, ISSN 0953-4822).